EMBROIDERY
Treasures

Craftworld Books

Contents

EMBROIDERY 4

LAVENDER AND MONTVILLE
ROSE BOW HANDTOWEL 8

JULIE'S PANSIES 12

TAKING FLOWERS TO MUMMY 17

CANDLEWICKED LAVENDER SACHETS 22

PRAIRIE SKY GRAPE URN 28

CHERUB ROSE URN 31

HOME PADDOCK BLANKET 34

FAIRY FLOSS PINCUSHION 38

DIAMONDS AND ROSES 44

HAPPY BIRTHDAY CAKE BAND 50

HAPPY EASTER BOOKMARK
AND GREETING CARD 53

PASTEL BLOSSOMS	57
BUSY BEE CHATELAINE	61
RING OF ROSES	65
CHERRY PINK PLACEMAT	69
VICTORIAN SILHOUETTES	73
FORGET-ME-NOT TAPE MEASURE COVER	76
NATIVE DELIGHTS	80
THE BASIC ESSENTIALS	84
STITCH GUIDE	88
INDEX	94

Embroidery

Embroidery is practised across the world and is one of the oldest textile crafts. Today, the art of embroidery and cross stitch is again increasing in popularity and, from ceremonial garments, both secular and ecclesiastical, to everyday clothes, carpets, and household linen, embroidery has certainly left its mark. What started out as a practical measure has turned into a highly skilled way of embellishing furnishings, fabrics, garments and more.

In medieval Byzantium, court garments and religious vestments were embroidered in rich colours and ornate designs. It did not take very long in the development of civilisation before stitching emerged as a decorative art form. Greek fabrics dating back to the 4th century BC, have been found embellished with satin and chain stitches.

The Romans referred to the art as 'painting with a needle' which reveals how highly they valued it. In ancient Greece, linen panels were embroidered in colourful silk, with geometric and floral patterns. In other parts of Europe, embroidery was used as a means of enriching clothing, church decorations, wall-hangings and domestic linens and furnishings.

In the centuries since, an enjoyment of embroidery has been shared by the wealthy upper classes and the poorest peasants. The fabrics on which they stitched differed – the rich working on satins and silks and the poor on coarsely woven cloths. Those who had ample leisure time stitched all sorts of furnishings and clothing, while those with less time and fewer materials embroidered specifically for a wedding trousseau or other special festivity. Regional differences arose, such as the use of small mirror pieces in Indian needlework, while foreign trading brought many local techniques to different countries.

During the British Tudor era, embroidery prospered as a domestic craft. Working furnishings for the great country houses became a major endeavour for the women of the household, and to be skilled with a needle was a vital accomplishment for a lady.

Chinese embroidery was principally used only to decorate garments for the elite, such as the celebrated and well-preserved robes of the many emperors adorned with traditional dragon motifs and other symbols of power, often worked on a dark silk.

By the 18th century, embroidery flourished throughout the world. In the east, the silk designs on Japanese kimonos displayed a level of skill hitherto unmatched, while in Europe, fashionable costumes for both men and women were decorated with fine embroidery.

The discovery of new lands led to an upsurge of interest in the exotic plants and flowers found there. As a result, images of the newly discovered species were copied from books and adorned the gowns of wealthy courtiers.

During the 19th century, the Victorians practised and enjoyed a wide range of embroidery styles such as stunning samplers and exquisite alphabets. Fine and delicate white-on-white embroidery was used on underwear and household linens, and among the peasants and artisans too, traditional techniques continued to be popular and were passed on from one generation to the next.

In the 1960s, British embroidery began an unprecedented development which saw the craft being widely practised and studied in colleges and schools. Skills have been enhanced and modern technology has produced such innovations as machine embroidery.

Embroidery continues to develop and grow well into the new millennium and beyond.

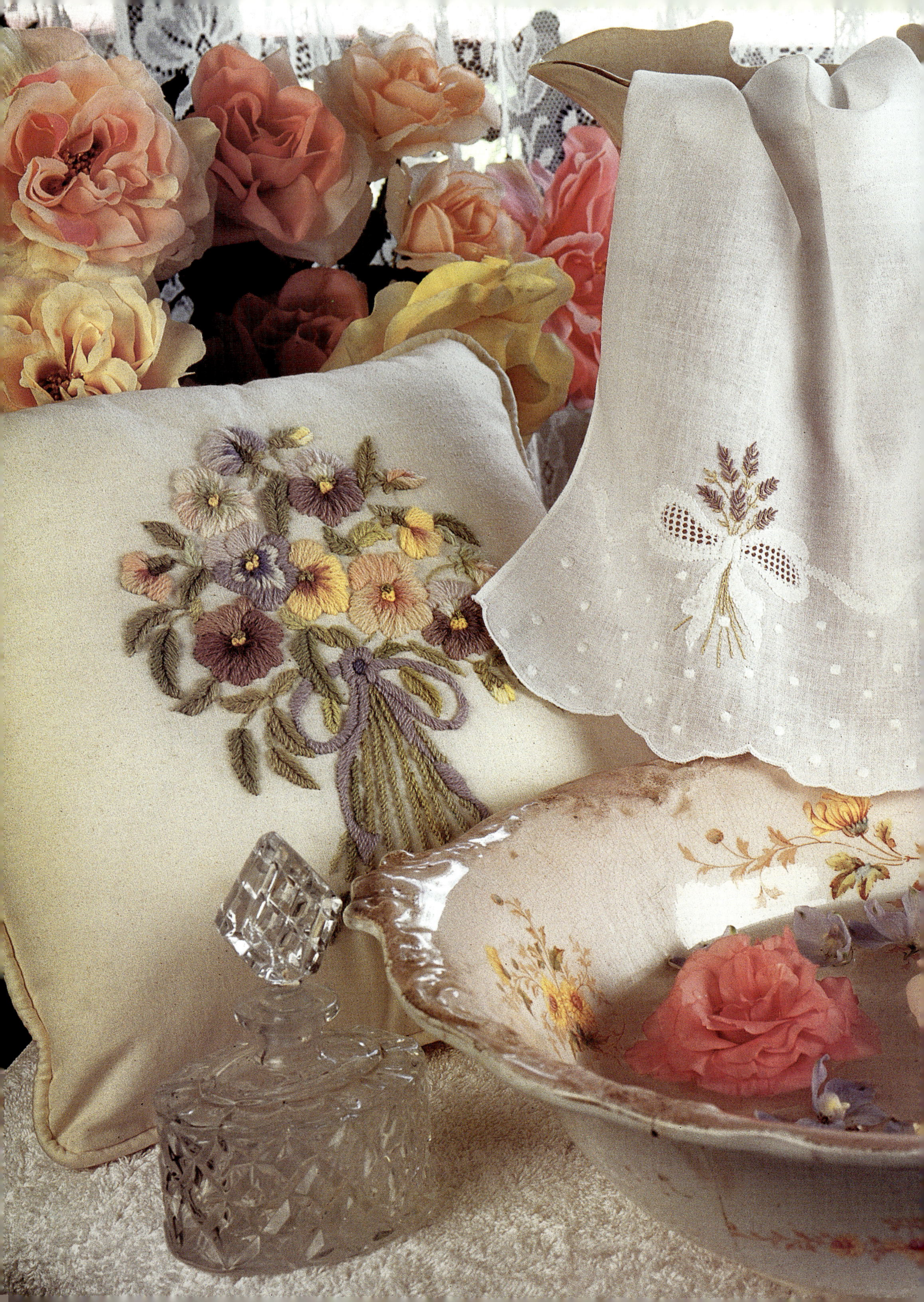

Pocketful of Posies

Lavender and Montville Rose Bow Handtowels

Your guests will feel especially welcome in your home when greeted with these simply stunning handtowels! Angela Watson has embellished some elegant purchased linen towels with two exquisite posies of delicate flowers.

MATERIALS

- 2 linen handtowels with a bow motif
- Madeira Mouline Embroidery Cotton:
- Lavender handtowel; one packet each of 1510, 2612
- Rose handtowel; one packet each of 0501, 0502, 0503, 1510
- No 9 crewel needle
- No 9 milliner's needle
- HB pencil

DESIGN SIZE

Lavender: 4cm x 8.5cm (1 1/2in x 3 3/8in)

Montville rose: 5cm x 10.5cm (2in x 4 1/8in)

STITCHES USED

Bullion Stitch, Lazy Daisy Stitch, Smocker's Knot, Stem Stitch, Straight Stitch

PREPARATION

❖

Using your preferred method of transfer, trace the design from the pattern sheet onto the handtowel with the sharp pencil. Use a soft light stroke, ensuring the tip of the pencil stays sharp and gives a fine, pale line.

EMBROIDERY

❖

As both sides of the handtowels will be visible and they must be regularly laundered, it is important not to carry any threads across the back of your work.

Lavender: Begin and finish each section of stitching with a Smocker's Knot on the back of the fabric. Refer to diagram 1 and thread two strands of (2612) cotton in the No 9 milliner's needle, then work a nine-wrap Bullion Stitch for the tip of the lavender. Work six more nine-wrap Bullion Stitches in pairs angled onto the stem. Using one strand of (1510) cotton in the No 9 crewel needle, place a loose Straight Stitch between each Bullion Stitch. Add two Lazy Daisy Stitches at the base of the lavender flower and continue in the same thread to work the stem in Stem Stitch. One stalk of lavender has no flowers – just three Lazy Daisy Stitches at the tip of the Stem-stitched stem. Use one strand of (1510) cotton and complete the stems below the linen bow in Stem Stitch.

Rose: The roses are worked in two strands of cotton in the No 9 milliner's needle and the foliage in one strand of (1510) cotton in the No 9 crewel needle.

Diagram 1 – *The lavender*

- Bullion Stitch
- Straight Stitch
- Lazy Daisy Stitch
- Stem Stitch

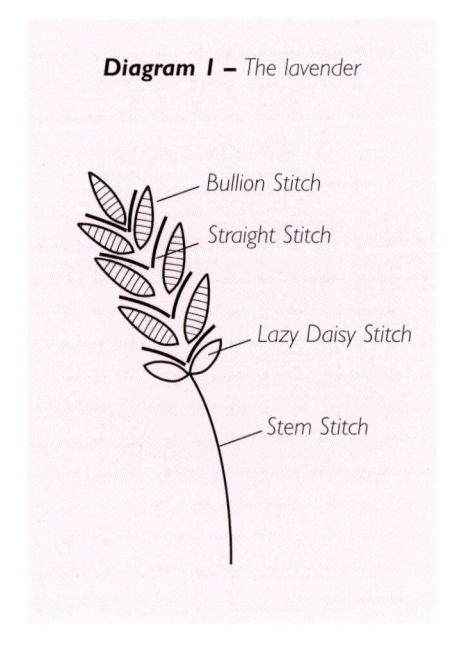

Each design is a mirror image of the other and consists of four large roses, five smaller roses and six buds.

Begin each large rose with two, five-wrap Bullion Stitches side by side in (0503) cotton, surround these with three, nine-wrap Bullion Stitches in (0502) cotton and finally, add the outer layer of six, 10-wrap Bullion Stitches in (0501) cotton. The smaller roses are worked in the same manner as the large roses but without the outer layer of petals. Stitch the centre in (0503) cotton, and the second layer in (0502) cotton. The centre of the bud is an eight-wrap Bullion Stitch in (0503) cotton, with two Bullion Stitches in (0502) cotton stitched to meet at the base of the bud and leave a third of the centre Bullion Stitch exposed at the tip.

Work an uneven Fly Stitch at the top of the bud and another Fly Stitch surrounding it as the calyx. Embroider the scattered leaves in Lazy Daisy Stitch and work two more Lazy Daisy Stitches at the base of each rose to form the calyxes. Complete the design with Stem Stitch to work the stems below the linen bow.

FINISHING

❖

Trim any thread tails, then dampen and spray-starch the handtowel. Place the embroidered side down on a thick towel and press it with a hot iron until dry.

For further information, contact Angela Watson, PO Box 238, Buddina QLD 4575, phone (07) 5444 0024 or email her at aawatson@ powerup.com.au ★

Lavender and Montville Rose

Julie's Pansies

One of the easiest ways to create a delightful garden is by embroidering one! The clever girls at Liz and Pauline Designs show us how to capture forever the happy faces of pansies.

PREPARATION

❖

Cut two 38cm (15in) squares of homespun for the cushion front and back and sufficient strips 5cm (2in) wide to make a length of 1.5m (1⅝yd) to cover the piping cord.

Using your preferred light source, trace the design outline from the pattern sheet onto one of the squares of homespun with the water-soluble marking pen.

Place the fabric into the embroidery hoop and pull it taut. It is wise to remove your work from the hoop when not stitching to avoid marks and the possibility of the fabric stretching.

HINTS FOR WOOL EMBROIDERY

❖

To thread the needle, loop the wool firmly around the needle and crease it. Then holding the crease between your finger and thumb push the eye of the needle down over the crease of the wool. Begin your stitching with a knot until there is sufficient embroidery worked to allow you to weave the wool through the back of the completed stitches to begin and end off. Do not carry the wool across the back of your work, but instead weave it through the back of the stitches already worked to the new stitch location.

EMBROIDERY

❖

Use two strands of wool for the embroidery unless stated otherwise.

The bow is worked in (891) wool in Satin Stitch, with the centre in (893).

Follow diagram 1 carefully for the correct placement of the colours used on the various leaves and posy stems, and work these in Slanted Satin Stitch. The smallest stems within the head of the posy are stitched in only one strand of (542) in Stem Stitch.

Pansies: Many of the flowers are built up with layers of colours. These particular petals have overlaid contrast colours which are marked on the individual flower diagrams. Each petal is first stitched with the background colour in Satin Stitch that extends over the entire petal from the outside edge to the centre. The first contrast colour is stitched over the background colour with the second contrast colour worked on top but having shorter stitches. These contrasting stitches are Straight Stitch that radiates from the centre. The plain petals are worked in Satin Stitch over the entire petal. The pansy flowers are individually numbered in diagram 1 and the thread guide for the stitching of each pansy is in diagram 2. Work each pansy in Satin Stitch, completing the entire petal background before working the contrasting layers of stitching at the centre. French Knots in (253) are worked at the very centre and the space underneath is filled with French Knots in (553).

MATERIALS

- 50cm x 90cm (19¾in x 36in) best quality seeded homespun
- Appleton's Crewel Embroidery Wool: one skein each of 141, 251, 251A, 252, 253, 351, 353, 354, 471, 473, 541, 542, 553, 601, 603, 701, 707, 711, 712, 714, 751, 753, 755, 841, 872, 874, 877, 883, 891, 893, 992, 996
- 1.5m (1⅝yds) piping cord
- No 22 chenille needle
- Size 14 cushion insert
- Cream sewing-machine thread
- Water-soluble marking pen
- 25cm (10in) embroidery hoop
- 34cm (13½in) square piece of cardboard

DESIGN SIZE

34cm (13½in) square

STITCHES USED

French Knots, Satin Stitch, Slanted Satin Stitch, Stem Stitch, Straight Stitch

EMBROIDERY TREASURES

Diagram 2 – *Pansy colours*
(Refer to diagram 1 for the placement of each pansy)

A — 141, 712, 711, 714, 711, 711

B — 877, 874, 253, 877/751, 877, 877/751

877/751 is one strand of 877 and one strand of 751 in the same needle

C — 841, 473, 471, 755, 471, 471

D — 707, 701, 753, 755, 701, 701, 701

E — 351, 542, 354, 471, 753, 471, 841, 755

F — 707, 753, 701, 707, 755

G — 883, 603, 992, 601, 601, 601

H — 996, 996, 872, 996, 996

I — 893, 883, 891, 354, 542, 253, 351, 351

J — 874, 253, 874, 877, 877/751

K — 753, 541, 701, two small stitches in 755

L — 351, 996, 872, 542, 541

M — 883, 883, 891, 891, 891, 992, 893

N — 542, 351, 541, 996, 872

Flower centres are French Knots in 253
Fill space with French Knots in 553

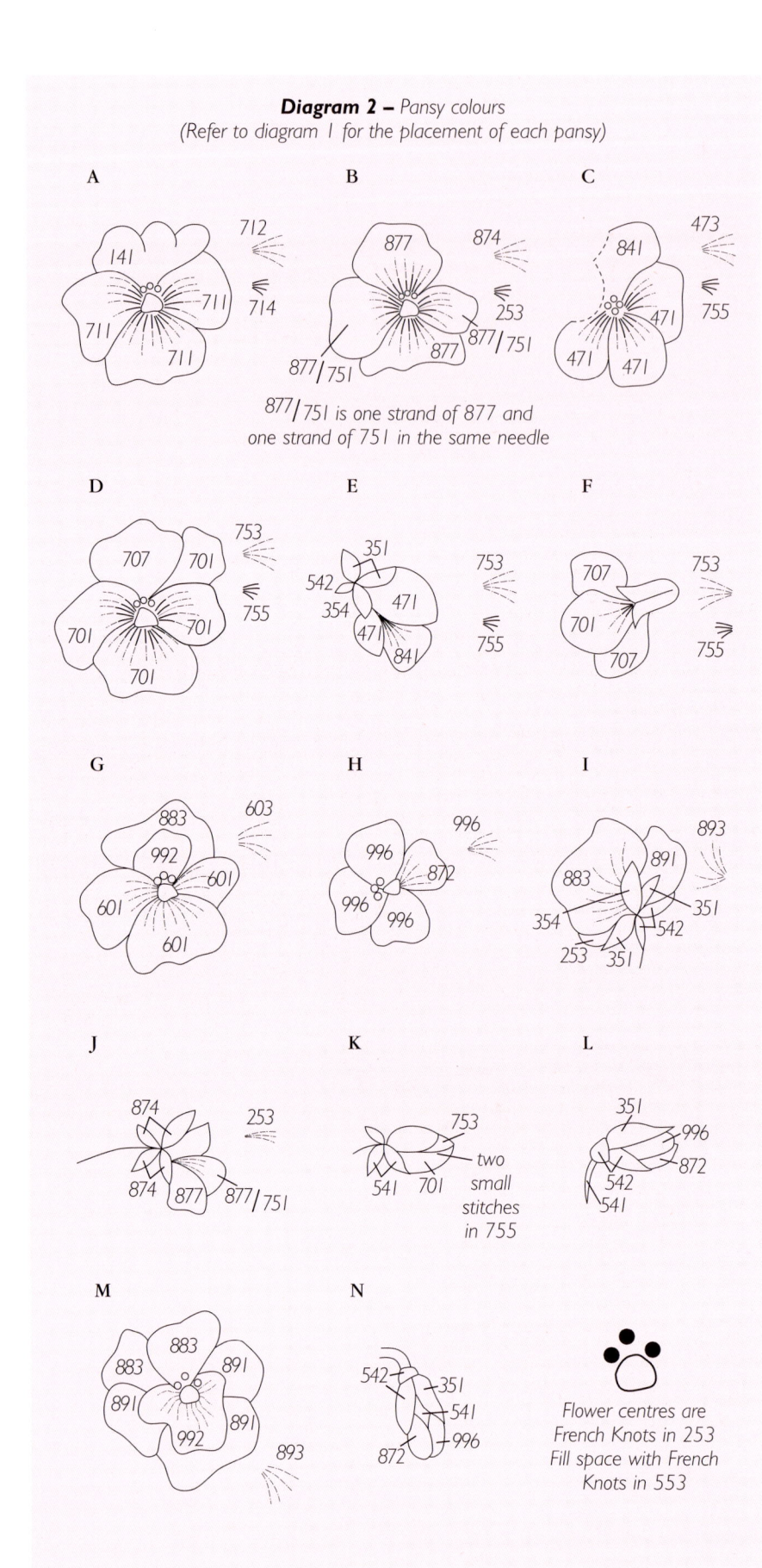

Pansy B has two petals stitched with a blend of colours. One strand of (877) and one strand of (751) are threaded in the needle at the same time to give the two petals a lovely mellow shade of pink. This technique and the same two colours are also used in pansy J. When stitching the first contrast layer on pansy M in (992) wool, make some of the stitches longer and go into the background petal stitching in (891) wool before working the centre Straight Stitches in colour (893).

FINISHING

❖

When the embroidery is completed remove any visible blue pen marks with a dab of water.

Make a cardboard template 34cm (13^{1}/$_{2}$in) square and round off the corners. Centre the template over the wool embroidery and trace around the edge.

Using the zipper foot on your sewing machine and cream sewing-machine thread, enclose the piping cord in the long strip of homespun fabric and stitch close to it to create the piping. A helpful hint when sewing with thick piping cord is to wrap the cord ends in sticky tape and cut through both the cord and the tape to achieve a clean-cut end. The cord will then not fray and the ends will abut together exactly.

Beginning in the centre of one side, pin the piping to the cushion front along the drawn line, remembering to clip the corners well to ensure the piping will spread out around the curve. Where the two ends of the piping meet, abut the cord together and fold one end of the piping fabric over the other to create a neat finish.

Place the backing square of homespun over the front, right sides together and pin or tack it securely.

Diagram 1 – Colours for the leaves and stems, and codes for pansy diagrams

Stitch around the edge, enclosing the piping and leaving a 20cm (8in) opening on the side opposite the join in the piping. Trim the seam allowance to around 1cm (3/8in) and turn the cushion right side out. Insert the cushion filler and slip-stitch the opening closed.

For further information, contact Liz and Pauline Designs, 18 Hornsby Street, Malvern Vic 3144, phone (03) 9822 5794. ✭

Taking Flowers to Mummy

What mother has not had a tear in her eye when her precious little child presents her with flowers gathered from the garden? These tokens of love are the priceless memories every parent holds dear and the inspiration for this magnificent embroidery by Robyn Rich.

MATERIALS

- 70cm (28in) square of best quality seeded homespun
- DMC Stranded Embroidery Cotton: two skeins each of very light shell pink (224), ultra very light shell pink (225); one skein each of ecru, white (Blanc), light hazelnut brown (422), light fern green (523), very light grey green (928), light brown grey (3023), light antique violet (3042), medium pine green (3363)
- Plaid Folk Art Acrylic Paint: Italian Sage (467), Settler's Blue (607), Rose Chiffon (753), Acorn Brown (941)
- ZIG Textile marker: brown, double-ended (encre pigment ink)
- Mill Hill Glass Seed Beads: 20, pink (00145) beads
- No 8 crewel Needle
- No 9 milliner's needle
- Fine-tipped paint brush
- 38cm (15in) embroidery hoop
- Soft lead pencil
- Plate
- Plastic wrap

DESIGN SIZE

22cm x 23cm (8⅝in x 9in)

STITCHES USED

Bullion Stitch, French Knot, Fly Stitch, Lazy Daisy Stitch, Stem Stitch, Straight Stitch

PREPARATION FOR PAINTING

❖

Press the homespun with a warm iron. Using your preferred light source, gently trace the outline of the design from the pattern sheet with the soft lead pencil, ensuring that the grain of the fabric is straight over the design outline.

PAINTING

❖

These paints are not colour-fast, however a fabric medium can be mixed with them to overcome this. To create a palette, cover a plate with plastic wrap and place dabs of the full-strength paint on it. Dip your brush in clean water and mix it with the paint until the desired colour and consistency is reached. If at any stage of the painting, the fabric appears too wet and needs more paint, place a piece of fabric over the homespun and press with a warm iron. This should also be done between changes of colour. Keep the brush as dry as possible to prevent the paint from running, and always test the colour and consistency on a scrap of the fabric. Using the brush end of the textile marker, very lightly mark the outlines of the children and add some shading on the ground.

Paint the straw hats in very diluted Acorn Brown (941), adding a little darker paint to the bottom of each hat for shading, and on the crown and brim. Paint the boy's shirt in the diluted paint adding shading under the arms and where the hat would cast a shadow.

Paint the shoes, making the sole of the girl's shoe darker and also shading one side of each shoe. Dilute the paint significantly to create a pleasing flesh colour and apply it to the arms and the girl's ankle. The ground is painted in diluted brown with a darker shade under the children and plants.

Dilute the Rose Chiffon (753) paint and apply it to the darker areas of the dress and hat bow first before diluting it more and painting the paler sections. The shading is to give a feeling of movement to the girl's dress.

Dilute the Settler's Blue (607) paint and apply it to the overalls, again shading areas that require it.

Paint the fine line of the forget-me-not vine, the plants and their stems in the full colour of Italian Sage (467), then dilute the paint and work the bushes and shading with tiny dabs. The climbing rose in the corner above the children's hands has the paint diluted, using it at its darkest in the corners and gradually making the dabs lighter towards the middle of the fabric.

Where there is the outline of a plant, carefully apply very diluted paint to give a soft shaded effect.

EMBROIDERY TIPS

❖

When stitching the embroidery, work with a piece of thread around 46cm (18in) as any longer will twist, knot and become unmanageable. Always separate the individual strands of the embroidery cotton and then regroup them into the number of strands to be used.

Place your work in a hoop to keep the embroidery taut and avoid carrying threads across the back as this can cause shadows on the front of the work and puckers in the fabric.

EMBROIDERY

❖

Girl's sunhat: Thread the No 9 milliner's needle with two strands of the very light shell pink (224) cotton and work double-wrap French Knots dotted evenly around the crown of the hat. Repeat this with ecru cotton and finally fill any spaces with more French Knots in light brown grey (3023).

Refer to diagram 1 for the flowers.

Lavender bush: Using two strands of light antique violet (3042) in the No 9 milliner's needle, work each lavender spike as a series of Lazy Daisy Stitches worked in pairs with the exception of the single stitch at the tip. Between 11 to 15 stitches may be needed to fill each flower spike. Complete the stems in Straight Stitch with two strands of light brown grey (3023).

Daisy bush: Work each daisy flower as five Lazy Daisy Stitches in two strands of white cotton in the No 8 crewel needle. Using two strands of light hazelnut brown (422), work a single double-wrap French Knot in the centre of each daisy. Add some incomplete daisy flowers to give the bush a realistic appearance. On the lower left half of the bush, work Lazy Daisy Stitches to form the leaves in two strands of medium pine green (3363) and complete the remaining leaves with two strands of light fern green (523).

Foxgloves: Stitch the centre foxglove first as a series of French Knots, in two strands of very light shell pink (224) in the No 9 milliner's needle. Complete the stem in Straight Stitch using two strands of light fern green (523), working four Lazy Daisy Stitches for the leaves at the base of the plant. Stitch the other two dark foxgloves and finally work the small paler flower in two strands of ultra very light shell pink (225).

Pink flowers: Make two Lazy Daisy Stitches in two strands of ultra very light shell pink (224) in the No 8 crewel needle to form the head of each flower. Stitch the stems with two strands of light brown grey (3023) in Stem Stitch and the leaves in Lazy Daisy Stitch.

Foliage: Thread the No 9 milliner's needle with two strands of the medium pine green (3363) and work a mass of French Knots, varying the number of wraps for added texture, underneath the lavender bush. Add some under the foxglove in the centre, then change to two strands of white cotton and stitch French Knots beneath the pink flowers on the left and in the centre of the embroidery. Working with two strands of light antique violet (3042), stitch French Knots in the lower right corner and a few

Diagram 1 – The flowers

Lavender

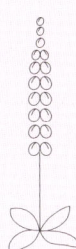

Foxglove

Pink flowers

Diagram 2 – The cream border

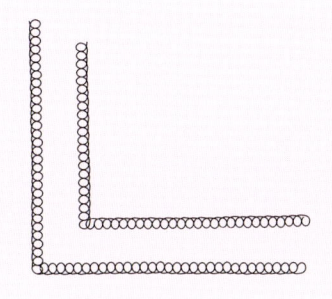

Step 1
Work the borders as French Knots in ecru cotton.

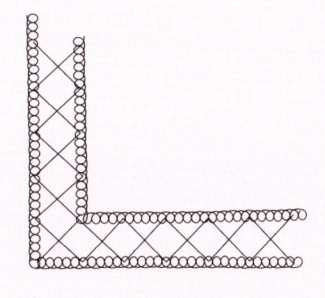

Step 2
Stitch crossed Straight Stitches in ecru between the borders.

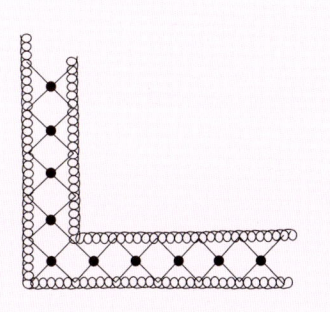

Step 3
Place a pink French Knot in the centre of each cross.

left of centre in the grass in light brown grey (3023).

Forget-me-not vine: Using one strand of very light grey green (928), work five double-wrap French Knots to form each flower, then use one strand of light hazelnut brown (422) to stitch a double-wrap French Knot in the centre.

Boy's lavender: The lavender in the boy's mouth is stitched in the same manner as the lavender bush using the same threads.

Green border: The green border below the forget-me-not vine, is a series of double-wrap French Knots in one strand of light fern green (523). The border inside the vine is stitched in the same manner, but not until the climbing rose is completed.

Climbing rose: This is composed of roses, half-open buds, closed buds and foliage in the top right and left corners above the children. These may be placed according to taste with the photograph as a guide only. Use the No 9 milliner's needle for all Bullion Stitches and French Knots. To work the roses, begin with two, six-wrap Bullion Stitches in two strands of very light shell pink (224), and then add three surrounding 15-wrap Bullion Stitches in ultra very light shell pink (225) to form the outer petals. The centres of the half-open buds are each two, six-wrap Bullion Stitches in two strands of very light shell pink (225). The closed buds are two, six-wrap Bullion Stitches in ultra very light shell pink (224). Thread the needle with two strands of light brown grey (3023) and add a calyx to each bud, open and closed, in Fly Stitch before scattering Lazy Daisy-stitched leaves throughout the climbing rose. Using the same colour, work French Knots to fill any areas that need it, varying the number of wraps to create texture.

Cream border: Refer to diagram 2 and work the two squares with two strands of ecru cotton to stitch the single-wrap French Knots placing them closely together to form a single line of knots. In between these two rows, work crossed Straight Stitches with two strands of ecru cotton and place a double-wrap French Knot in very light pale pink (224) cotton in the centre of each cross.

The stunning rose border that surrounds this embroidery consists of roses, open buds, half-open buds and closed buds. Refer to diagram 3. With the exception of the open buds, follow the specific instructions for these flowers in the climbing rose as they are worked in the same manner. The open bud has two central six-wrap Bullion Stitches worked in two strands of very light shell pink (224) cotton, then two outer eight-wrap Bullion Stitches and two more six-wrap Bullion Stitches, the last four in two strands of ultra very light shell pink (225) cotton. These six stitches are all worked in a row and not a spiral. Follow the diagram for the placement of the roses, buds and foliage on the outer border. Thread the No 8 crewel needle with two strands of the light brown grey (3023) cotton and work a calyx around every bud in Fly Stitch. Using the same colour, stitch the leaves in Lazy Daisy Stitches and add the single-wrap French Knots scattered amongst the flowers. Single-wrap French Knots in two strands of both ecru cotton and very light shell pink (224) cotton are also stitched in the border.

Bead border: Attach each pink (00145) bead firmly with a single strand of ultra very light pale pink (225) cotton and secure the thread on the back. Do not carry the thread from one bead to the next, as it will be visible on the front.

FINISHING

❖

Place the embroidery right side down on a firm surface and trim any thread tails, before pressing with a warm iron. Your embroidery is now ready to be professionally framed to give you many hours of pleasure.

For further information, contact Robyn Rich Creations, PO Box 275, Crib Point Vic 3919, phone (03) 5983 9393 or email Robyn at robyn@richcreations.com.au ✮

Diagram 3 –
The rose border
Work the rose border around the four sides

Rose

Open bud with calyx

Half-open bud with calyx

Closed bud with calyx

Leaves in Lazy Daisy Stitch

Candlewick Lavender Sachets

Hearts and flowers are firm favourites with embroiderers and Marian Edwards' candlewicked sachets for holding potpourri are sure to enchant you. Perhaps you might like to fill yours with chocolates for a different touch.

MATERIALS

- 30cm x 70cm (12in x 28in) calico or quilter's muslin
- 65cm x 4cm (26in x 1½in) cotton lace
- DMC Maeva 10 crochet cotton: one ball
- No 20 chenille needle
- 1m (1⅛yd) wire-edged ribbon
- 14cm x 60cm (5½in x 23¾in) batting
- Cream sewing-machine thread
- No 20 chenille needle
- Small amount of polyester filling
- Potpourri
- Lead pencil
- 10cm (4in) embroidery hoop (optional)

DESIGN SIZE

13cm x 30cm (5⅛in x 12in)

STITCHES USED

Colonial Knot, Cretan Stitch, Double Knot Stitch, Feather Stitch

PREPARATION

Do not wash the calico until all the embroidery is completed. Cut the calico into four rectangles each measuring 16.5cm x 29cm (6⅝in x 11½in). Find the centre of the two fronts by folding them in half vertically and finger-pressing the fold. Place a pin 5cm (2in) up from the lower raw edge along the centre to mark the base of the embroidery design. Using your preferred light source, trace each design on the pattern sheet onto the calico with the lead pencil. Ensure no part of the design extends past the marking pin.

EMBROIDERY

The embroidery is worked with 30cm (12in) lengths of the crochet cotton in the No 20 chenille needle. Use a single thread throughout except for the Colonial Knots which are worked in a double thread, and you may choose to use a small embroidery hoop to hold the calico securely.

Refer to diagram 1 for the placement of the different embroidery stitches on each of the two designs. Begin the heart design using Feather Stitch to work the inner heart and the scrolls at the top of the pattern. Complete the outer heart and scrolls at the bottom in Double Knot Stitch and the four small motifs in Cretan Stitch. Change to a double thread of crochet cotton and stitch the five clusters of four Colonial Knots.

Begin the floral design with Feather Stitch to work the four central petals. Fill the small petals between these with closely packed Cretan Stitch, then work their outlines in Feather Stitch. Complete the four pairs of scrollwork in Double Knot Stitch, before again changing to a double thread and working the four Colonial-knot clusters and the seven Colonial Knots in the design centre.

FINISHING

When all of the embroidery is completed, wash all four pieces of calico in warm soapy water. Rinse them well then place them in a bowl and cover them with boiling water straight from the kettle. Leave them to soak for 15 minutes. This shrinking technique is unique to candlewicking and may even enhance your embroidery. Complete the shrinking process prior to making up the sachets as a shrinkage of up to 2cm (¾in) is to be expected. After the final rinse, pull the calico gently into shape and dry it flat. Iron it face down onto a white fluffy towel while still slightly damp, and again gently pull it into shape.

Diagram 1 – *Sachet embroidery placement*

FLORAL MOTIF

- Double Knot Stitch
- Cretan Stitch
- Colonial Knots
- Feather Stitch

HEART MOTIF

- Feather Stitch
- Cretan Stitch
- Double Knot Stitch
- Colonial Knots

Pin the embroidered front to the back, right sides together and stitch the sides and base with a 1cm (3/8in) seam allowance before overlocking to neaten the edges. Turn a 1cm (3/8in) hem under along the top edge of the sachet. Cut the lace to fit each sachet and join the raw edges with French seams before pinning it in place. Carefully zigzag the lace to the top of the sachets and press them carefully with a hot iron, particularly near the seams. Cut the batting in half and make two inserts filled with the potpourri and the polyester filling. Place one inside each sachet and tie them closed with the ribbon.

For further information, contact Marian Edwards, PO Box 310, Moe VIC 3825, phone (03) 5127 2784 or email her at marian@vic.australis.com.au ✯

EMBROIDERY TREASURES — *Candlewick Lavender Sachets*

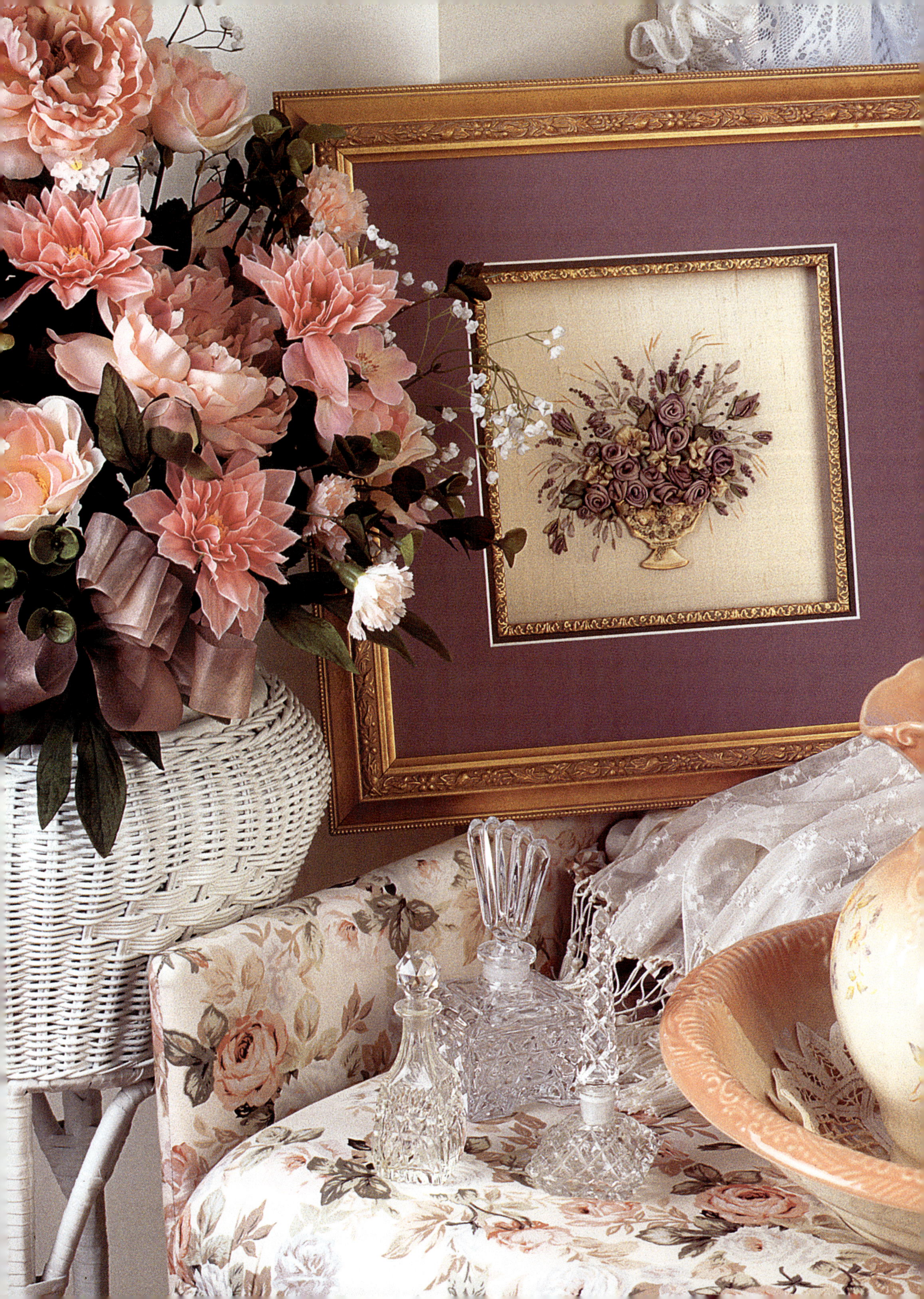

Beautiful Bouquets

Prairie Sky Grape Urn

Christine Sumner has adorned an ornate urn with sumptuous silk ribbons in hues of dusky lilacs to create an everlasting floral memory.

PREPARATION

❖

Using a light box or a bright sunlit window, trace the design outline on the pattern sheet onto the silk with the marking pen. Overlock the edges of the silk to prevent them fraying. Place the Pellon on the back of the silk, tack around the edges, and run a vertical and horizontal line of tacking through the centre of the fabric. Place the piece in the embroidery hoop and tighten it firmly.

EMBROIDERY

❖

Roses: Make 13 Folded Ribbon Roses with the 15mm ($^5/8$in) prairie sky ribbon, using the No 9 milliner's needle and matching sewing-machine thread to construct them. Then with the No 9 crewel needle, make an additional six Folded Ribbon Roses in the 7mm ($^1/4$in) (178) and (179) silk ribbons, laying the two ribbons together to vary the colour within each rose.

Following the traced design and photograph, attach the flowers to the silk with the No 7 milliner's needle.

Daisies: Thread the No 18 chenille needle with the 7mm ($^1/4$in) silk ribbon (51), and make the five daisies by working petals of seven Loop Stitches for each flower. Taking care not to pull the ribbon, fill the centre of each daisy with five single-wrap French Knots in autumn hydrangea in the No 5 milliner's needle.

Leaves: Using the No 18 chenille needle and 7mm ($^1/4$in) rosemary ribbon, work the leaves amongst the roses in Loop Stitch and five Lazy Daisy-stitch leaves around the roses. Add Loop-stitch leaves in the 4mm ($^1/8$in) rosemary ribbon in the No 20 chenille needle to give a variety of textures to the work.

Spray of buds: Begin each spray working from the roses outwards forming the groups of buds in Ribbon Stitch using the 4mm ($^1/8$in) ribbon (178) in the No 20 chenille needle. Change to a No 7 crewel needle and the (8E) medium silk thread and place a Fly Stitch around each bud following the lines of the design outline carefully, then complete the spray with a French Knot at the base of each bud in the (8E) silk.

Large buds: The two large buds are worked in the 7mm ($^1/4$in) (179) ribbon and No 18 chenille needle as a Lazy Daisy Stitch with a Ribbon Stitch over the top. Using the beading needle, attach nine of the mauve (6134) beads along the centre of the bud over the Ribbon Stitch. Work two Ribbon Stitches on each side, in the 4mm ($^1/8$in) rosemary ribbon and No 20 chenille needle, then complete the stem in Straight Stitch with the (8E) medium silk in the No 7 crewel needle.

Small buds: The seven small buds are stitched next using the No 18 chenille needle and the 7mm ($^1/4$in) (179) ribbon. Work a single Ribbon Stitch for each bud and attach seven of the mauve (6134) beads down the centre of the ribbon. Using the No 20 chenille needle and the 4mm ($^1/8$in) rosemary ribbon, work Ribbon Stitch around each of the seven small buds, then complete the stem in Straight Stitch with the (8E) medium silk and No 7 crewel needle.

Wisteria: Thread the No 5 milliner's needle with the autumn hydrangea thread and work the groups of French Knots. The stem is stitched in the same way as the large and small buds.

The final touches on the embroidery are the gold-coloured highlights and the extra beads. Work a series of 30-wrap Bullion Stitches in one strand of the baby camel (45) threaded in the beading needle and complete the stems of each spray in one strand of (8E) fine silk. Attach the mauve/green (9128) beads

MATERIALS

- 40cm x 50cm (16in 20in) cream silk Dupion
- Judith & Kathryn Designs grape urn
- Margot's High Twist Floriate Thread: one skein of autumn hydrangea
- Kacoonda Medium Silk: one packet of (8E)
- Kacoonda Fine Silk: one packet of (8E)
- Rajmahal Art Silk: one skein of baby camel (45)
- Margot's 15mm ($^5/8$in) Soft Satin Ribbon: 3m ($3^1/4$yd) prairie sky
- Petals 4mm ($^1/8$in) and 7mm ($^1/4$in) Silk Ribbons: one card of each in rosemary
- YLI 4mm ($^1/8$in) Silk Ribbon: 4m ($4^3/8$yd) of (178)
- YLI 7mm ($^1/4$in) Silk Ribbon: 3m ($3^1/4$yd) of (51) and (179); 1m ($1^1/8$yd) of (178)
- Maria George Beads: one packet each of mauve (6134), mauve/green (9128)
- 40cm x 50cm (16in x 20in) Pellon
- No 18, 20 and 22 chenille needles
- No 7 and 9 crewel needles
- No 5, 7 and 9 milliner's needles
- Beading needle
- Sewing-machine thread
- 25cm (10in) embroidery hoop
- Water-soluble marking pen
- Craft glue

DESIGN SIZE

15cm x 14cm (6in x 5$^1/2$in)

STITCHES USED

Bullion Stitch, Folded Ribbon Rose, French Knot, Fly Stitch, Lazy Daisy Stitch, Loop Stitch, Ribbon Stitch, Straight Stitch

to your work with the beading needle following the design outline for their placement.

FINISHING

❖

Make sure the marking pen has been removed and allow the silk to dry thoroughly before gluing the urn carefully in place.

Your magnificent urn overflowing with roses is now ready to be professionally framed.

For further information, contact Christine Sumner at Eliza Craft & Wool, 44 Mt Eliza Way, Mt Eliza Vic 3930, phone (03) 9787 6155. ✯

Cherub Rose Urn

*Christine Sumner's stunning bouquet of pink-toned flowers
in an urn skillfully held by cherubs evokes an image of romance,
friendship and love.*

MATERIALS

- Judith & Kathryn Designs double cherub urn
- 50cm (19³⁄₄in) square cream Silk Dupion
- Kacoonda Fine Silk: two packets of 101
- Kacoonda High Twist Silk: one packet of 101
- YLI 1000 Denier Silk Thread: one reel of 159
- Margot's 15mm (⁵⁄₈in) Soft Satin Ribbon: 6m (6¹⁄₂yd) brandy
- Petals 4mm (¹⁄₈in) Silk Ribbon: one packet each of copper rose and rosemary
- Petals 7mm (¹⁄₄in) Silk Ribbon: one packet of copper rose
- YLI 4mm (¹⁄₈in) Silk Ribbon: 2m (2¹⁄₄yd) of 143
- YLI 7mm (¹⁄₄in) Silk Ribbon: 6m (6⁵⁄₈yd) of 51; 5m (5¹⁄₂yd) of 52
- Mokuba 8mm (⁵⁄₁₆in) Ribbon No 4597: 1.5m (1⁵⁄₈yd) of green gold stripe (14)
- Mill Hill Glass Seed Beads: one packet of coral (00275)
- Mill Hill Antique Glass Beads: one packet of smokey heather (03031)
- No 16, 18, 20 and 22 chenille needles
- No 8 crewel needle
- No 5 milliner's needle
- Beading needle
- 50cm (20in) square Pellon
- 25cm (10in) embroidery hoop
- Water-soluble marking pen
- Craft glue

DESIGN SIZE

20cm x 18cm (8in x 7¹⁄₈in)

STITCHES USED

Bullion Stitch, Folded Ribbon Rose, French Knots, Fly Stitch, Lazy Daisy Stitch, Loop Stitch, Pistil Stitch, Ribbon Stitch

PREPARATION

❖

Overlock the edges of the silk fabric to prevent it fraying. Using a light box or a sunlit window, trace the pattern onto the silk using the water-soluble marking pen.

EMBROIDERY

❖

Using the 15mm (⁵⁄₈in) brandy ribbon, make 22 Folded Ribbon Roses and stitch them in place above the urn, making sure they are closely packed, then work the leaves in Loop Stitch using the (143) silk ribbon.

Large wisteria: Begin to work the three large wisteria flowers in the 4mm (¹⁄₈in) copper rose silk ribbon using the No 20 chenille needle. Make six Lazy Daisy Stitches as indicated in diagram 1, then change to the 4mm (¹⁄₈in) rosemary silk ribbon and place a Ribbon Stitch on either side of each Lazy Daisy Stitch. Using the (101) fine silk thread in the beading needle, work 20, 35-wrap Bullion Stitches, placing them in pairs around the flowers. Complete the base of the flower frond with two large Lazy Daisy Stitches in the green gold striped ribbon (14) in the No 16 chenille needle.

Daisies: Using the No 18 chenille needle and the 7mm (¹⁄₄in) copper rose ribbon, make five Lazy Daisy Stitches. Change to the No 20 chenille needle and add four or five French Knots in the centre using the 7mm (¹⁄₄in) silk ribbon (51).

French-knot clusters: Thread the No 18 chenille needle with the 7mm (¹⁄₄in) silk ribbon (51) and work the five clusters of French Knots. The number of knots in each cluster will vary from around 12 to 15. Using the High Twist (101) silk in the No 5 milliner's needle, work a French Knot in the centre of each of the ribbon French Knots.

Gold flowers: Each of the five flowers consists of two Lazy Daisy Stitches at the base using the No 18 chenille needle and the 7mm (¹⁄₄in) (52) silk ribbon, followed by two Pistil Stitches on each side in the same ribbon. Thread the No 5 milliner's needle with the (159) silk thread, and make five to six Pistil Stitches radiating out from the centre. Complete the flower with French Knots in the centre in the 4mm (¹⁄₈in) copper rose ribbon in the No 22 chenille needle.

Small wisteria: Using the High Twist (101) in the No 5 milliner's needle, create the four smaller wisteria in French Knots using double-wraps for the knots at the centre and single-wraps for those on the outer edge. Work Ribbon Stitch around the base of these using the green gold stripe ribbon (14) threaded in the No 16 chenille needle.

Beaded buds: Thread the No 18 chenille needle with the 7mm (¹⁄₄in) copper rose ribbon and work a Ribbon Stitch for each of the five buds. Attach five or six coral (00275) beads on top of the silk ribbon giving the bud the appearance of a peapod.

Scatter the smokey heather (03031) beads around the embroidery design.

FINISHING

❖

Glue the urn in place using a small amount of the craft glue and ensure the marking pen has been either covered with embroidery or erased with a damp cotton bud.

For further information, contact Christine Sumner at Eliza Craft & Wool, 44 Mt Eliza Way, Mt Eliza Vic 3930, phone (03) 9787 6155. ★

EMBROIDERY TREASURES — *Cherub Rose Urn*

Home Paddock Blanket

This is certainly the perfect blanket for a first adventure with wool embroidery. Jan McNeice has created these naughty sheep intent upon mischief in the garden, using the simplest of stitches to really tempt beginners – or even a new grandparent!

PREPARATION

❖

Straighten the piece of wool blanketing and remove any selvedges to avoid any distortion occurring after the blanket is bound. Place the tulle over the design outline on the pattern sheet and trace the design with the black marking pen. This becomes the permanent copy to transfer the design to the blanketing. When deciding on the placement of the design on the wool, remember to allow for the blanket to be tucked in at the bottom and turned over to show the backing at the top. Place the legs of the lowest sheep on the tulle 30cm (12in) from the bottom of the blanket and pin them securely in place. Using the water-soluble marking pen, trace over the outlines of the sheep and mark the stems and centres of the scattered flowers. If at anytime the markings disappear simply place the tulle over the design and transfer the details again.

EMBROIDERY

❖

Use one strand of wool throughout for the embroidery in the No 22 chenille needle.

Sheep: Using the Daisies (963) wool, Stem-stitch around the outside of the sheep's bodies omitting the feet and face. Fill the body with French Knots in Blossom (963) working systematically up and down the shape or across and back, then complete the face and feet on the sheep in Satin Stitches using (987).

Daisies: The daisies are worked in Lazy Daisy Stitch with a French-Knot centre. Begin with five evenly spaced Lazy Daisy Stitches in (853) that form a circle and add three or four French Knots in the centre in (742). Complete the cluster of daisies with a scattering of single Lazy Daisy-stitch leaves in (636).

Forget-me-nots: Using (387), stitch the forget-me-nots with five evenly spaced French Knots in a circle. Work the yellow centres as a single French Knot in (708), and the leaves in Lazy Daisy Stitches using (628).

Grape hyacinth: Begin with the stems in Straight Stitch using (625). Add the flowers in (AZ4) as four or five French Knots at the base of the flower spike, gradually tapering to one French Knot at the very tip.

Daffodils: Work the stems and leaves first in Stem Stitch in (628). The trumpet of each daffodil is stitched in

TIPS ON WOOL EMBROIDERY FOR BEGINNERS

❖

To begin the embroidery use a knot with a 1cm (3/8in) tail. To finish off, make several backstitches on the back of the embroidery and weave the tail through the other stitches. Make sure the needle chosen has a large enough eye so that the embroidery wool will not be damaged as it passes through the blanketing. Don't be tempted to use a long thread as it easily tangles and this causes wear on the thread – an ideal length is from the elbow to the index finger. When selecting the wools for a project, bunch them together to form a posy and see if they make a pleasing display. Any colours that don't blend should be obvious and an alternative can be selected.

When embroidering after using a water-soluble marking pen to outline the design, keep a damp white handkerchief nearby to remove any markings still visible as each section of the design is completed.

MATERIALS

- 60cm x 80cm (23 3/4in x 31 1/2in) pure wool blanketing
- 1m x 115cm (1 1/8yds x 45in) cotton print fabric for backing and binding
- Gumnut Blossoms Crewel Wool: two skeins of 963; one skein each of 387, 625, 628, 636, 708, 742, 744, 853, 987
- Gumnut Daisies Fine Wool: one skein of 963
- Gumnut Gemstones Crewel Wool: one skein each of AZ3, AZ4
- 30cm x 25cm (12in x 10in) white tulle
- No 22 chenille needle
- Black marking pen
- Water-soluble marking pen

DESIGN SIZE

60cm x 80cm (23 3/4in x 31 1/2in)

STITCHES USED

Buttonhole Stitch, French Knots, Lazy Daisy Stitch, Satin Stitch, Stem Stitch, Straight Stitch

(708) at the top of the stem. Begin with three elongated Buttonhole Stitches, bringing the stitches close to each other to form a bell, then add the petals at the top of the trumpet in (744) using Lazy Daisy Stitches.

Alyssum: To give the appearance of alyssum, work clumps of nine or more French Knots in a mix of (AZ3) and (742) wool, then scatter Straight-stitch leaves using (636) around the clumps of flowers.

Grass: Create the grass using Straight Stitches in a variety of lengths and directions. Vary the colour used throughout the embroidery from the selection of 625, 636 and 628.

Don't forget to embroider the date and your initials on your heirloom of tomorrow!

FINISHING

❖

Measure the blanket again and ensure it is straight and even. Cut the cotton print backing fabric to 71cm x 91cm (28in x 36in) to give the allowance for the 4cm (1¹/2in) binding and a 1.5 cm (⁵/8in) seam allowance. Press the seam allowance under on all four edges and also the 4cm (1¹/2in) binding. Centre the blanket with the embroidery side up on the wrong side of the print fabric.

Using large tacking stitches, tack a grid of lines through both layers to hold the two fabrics together securely. Fold the corners of the print fabric so the diagonal fold lies across the corner point of the blanket. Press the fold with the iron, then open out the print fabric so the pressed folds meet at the corner and machine-stitch them together on the fold line on the wrong side to form a mitre. Trim any excess fabric, then press the seam open and turn it right side out. Pin the binding in place and slip-stitch it to the blanketing. The blanket is now finished and ready for that new arrival.

For further information, contact Jan McNiece, phone (03) 9899 4085 or email her on howardjan@bigpond.com ✯

EMBROIDERY TREASURES — *Home Paddock Blanket*

Fairy Floss Pincushion

Does it remind you of light-as-air fairy floss at the fair? This colourful little pincushion by Judith Adams is as delightful to look at – and stitch – as your memories of a rainbow-coloured wand of spun sugar just waiting to be eaten!

MATERIALS

- 12cm x 60cm (4³/4in x 23³/4in) white cotton and linen blend fabric
- 1m x 6cm (1¹/8yd x 2³/8in) wide embroidered cotton netting
- Madeira Stranded Silk Embroidery Thread: one packet each of 0112, 1002, 1701
- 50cm (20in) white mini piping
- 12cm x 15cm (4³/4in x 6in) fusible lightweight interfacing
- 4 pink sequin pearl buttons
- No 8 crewel needle
- White sewing-machine thread
- Polyester filling
- Pins

DESIGN SIZE

62 pleats

8cm x 11cm (3¹/4in x 4³/8in)

STITCHES USED

Cable Stitch, Lazy Daisy Stitch, One-step Wave, Stair-step Wave

PREPARATION

❖

Cut the panel to be smocked to 12cm x 45cm (4³/4in x 18in), and use a smocking pleater such as the Amanda Jane to pleat the fabric with 11 full-space rows. It would be helpful to include as many half-space rows as possible but this is not essential. Steam the fabric on the pleater needles to give the pleats a sharp edge. This is a particularly useful technique when pleating silk, wool or linen – and linen blends. As the needles fill with fabric, steam the pleats, then pull the pleated fabric off the needles without flattening them and repeat the process until the entire pincushion is pleated. Allow a seam allowance at each end and remove the gathering threads from the pleats leaving exactly the 62 pleats required to smock the design given. Tie the threads off in pairs so that the pleated panel measures 11cm (4³/8in).

Many fine needlework stores provide a pleating service for personal shoppers as well as by mail order.

SMOCKING

❖

The design is worked in three strands of the silk thread. It is essential to 'strip' the thread – that is, remove each strand individually from the skein – then place three stands together and knot them. Follow the graph in diagram 1 carefully, noting that rows 1 and 11 are holding rows and are therefore not smocked. These help to keep the pleats neat and even during smocking and stitching the pincushion.

Diagram 1 – *Smocking design*

Holding Row

Row 1
Row 2
Row 3
Row 4
Row 5
Row 6
Row 7
Row 8
Row 9
Row 10

Holding Row

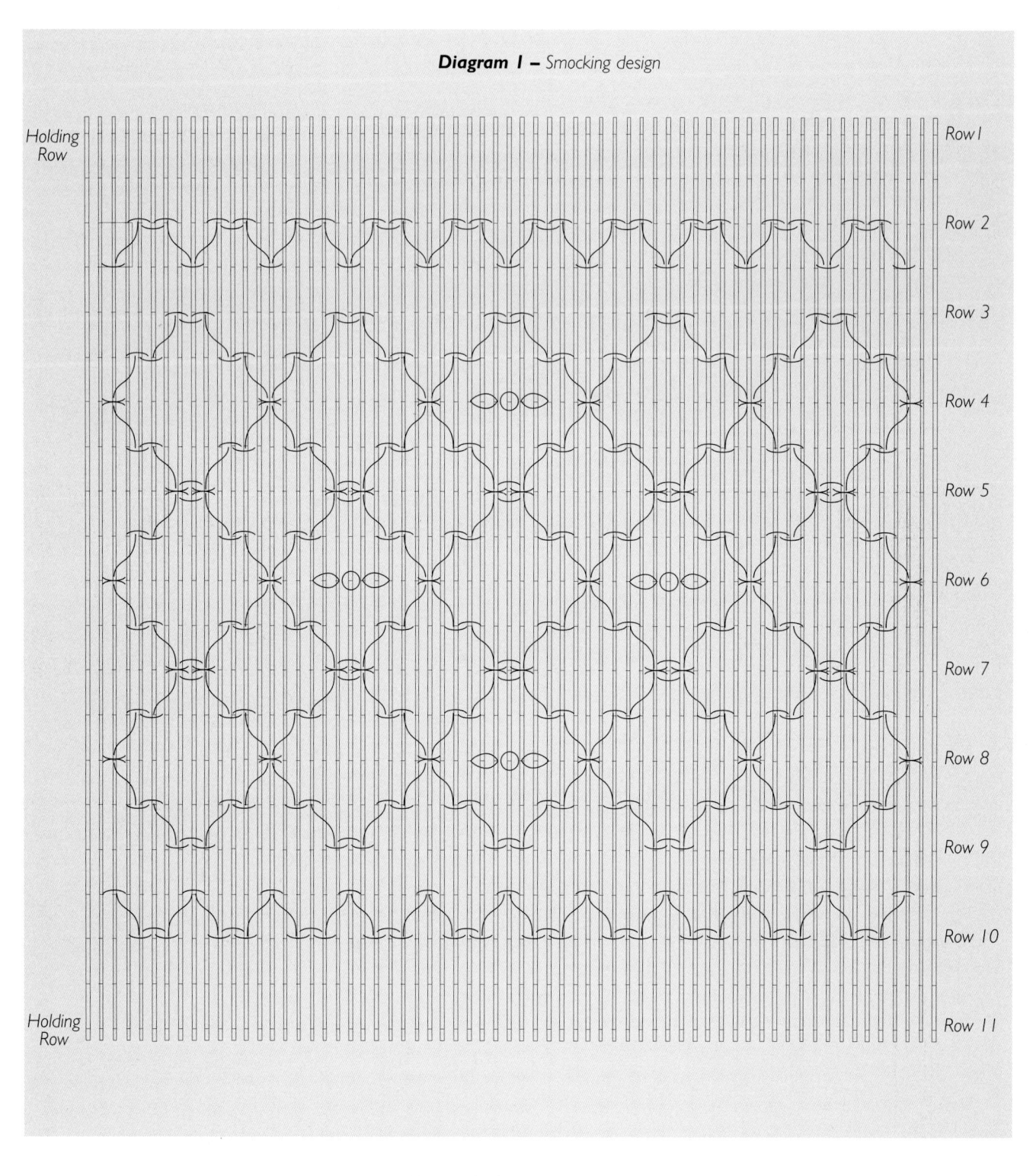

Row 11

Working with three strands of (0112) silk in the No 8 crewel needle, begin on row 2½ with a down Cable Stitch. Smock a One-step Wave to row 2 followed by three Cable Stitches, beginning with an up Cable Stitch, then a One-step Wave back to row 2½. This sequence is repeated across the panel to give 10 waves. Stitch the mirror image between row 9½ and row 10 in the same colour.

Begin on row 4 with three strands of (1002) silk and make a down Cable Stitch, followed by a Stair-step Wave to row 3 and back. To work the Stair-step

Wave, smock a One-step Wave to row $3^{1}/_{2}$ followed by an Up Cable Stitch, then a Down Cable Stitch. Continue with a One-step Wave to row 3 and smock three Cable Stitches, up, down, up, then a One-step Wave to row $3^{1}/_{2}$ with two Cable Stitches, down, up, and finish on row 4 with a Down Cable Stitch. There are five of these waves across the panel. The mirror image is stitched between rows 4 and 5.

The Stair-step Wave and its mirror image are also stitched between rows 5 and 7, and rows 7 and 9.

Stitch the four pink buttons in place and work a Lazy Daisy Stitch on both sides of each button in two strands of (1701) silk.

Pin the smocked panel to a padded surface such as the ironing board and steam it for about two minutes, holding the iron approximately 2.5cm (1in) above the stitching. This process is called blocking. Remove the gathering threads from the panel with the exception of rows 1, 2, 10 and 11. These will be removed after the piping is stitched in place.

FINISHING

❖

Turn the panel smocking side down on the ironing board and gently iron the fusible interfacing to the back. This will help the pincushion to hold its shape better after filling it with the polyester filling.

Pin the white piping in place around the smocked panel and stitch it in place. Remove any remaining pleating gathering threads. Join the embroidered netting into a circle and run two rows of machine-gathering stitches along the raw edge. Pull up the gathering threads and pin the netting in place next to the cord in the piping. It should be right side down touching the smocking when stitched in position. Trim the spare piece of fabric a little larger than the panel and place it on top over the netting and smocking and stitch all the layers together. Leave an opening along one of the longer sides to turn the pincushion right side out. Trim any seam allowances and overlock the raw edge before turning it through the opening and filling it with the polyester filling. Finally, neatly slip-stitch the opening closed and just enjoy your wonderfully colourful smocked pincushion.

For further information, contact The Status Thimble, 11 Leatherwood Court, Baulkham Hills NSW 2153, phone/fax (02) 9686 2713 or email adams@mt.net.au ✯

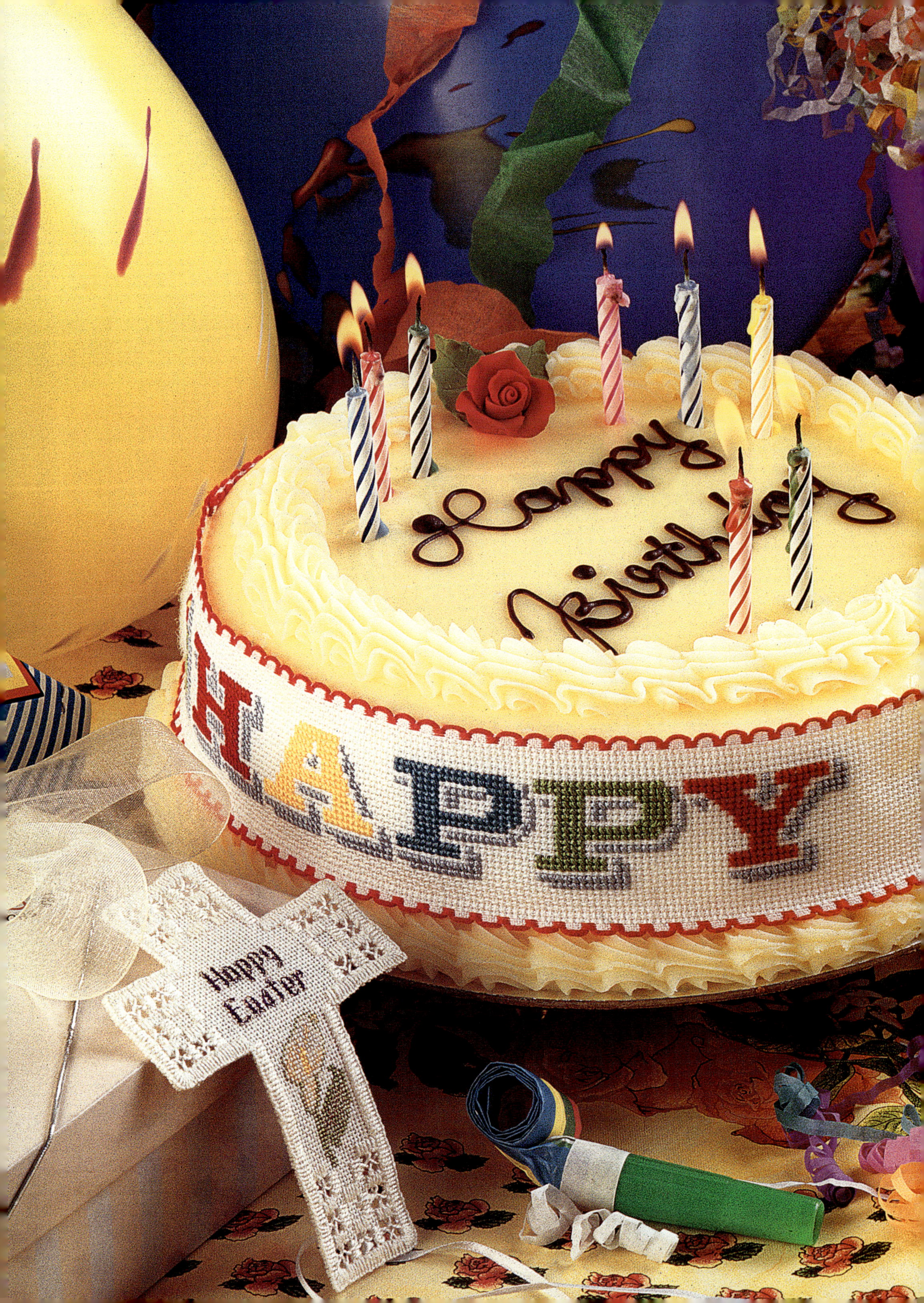
Happy Birthday
HAPPY
Happy Easter

Let's Celebrate

Diamonds and Roses

This stunning example of Brazilian embroidery designed and stitched by Debbie Kelley, a designer from the USA, was the result of a challenge she set herself. While Debbie discovered her talents quite by accident, this unique design will enable you to discover yours.

PREPARATION

❖

Fold the square piece of fabric in half then half again to find the centre. Centre the pattern from the pattern sheet, and lightly trace the design outline onto the fabric using a lightbox, or your preferred light source. It is important to keep all the tracing lines very light and fine as the Sadi is not washable.

Hint: Before stitching with the Art Silk, it is recommended that the thread be 'conditioned' by separating the strands and gently drawing each one across a slightly dampened sponge, before placing the desired number of strands together. This allows them to move independently for a smoother result. It may also be necessary to adjust the tension of all the strands to insure they are even before working your stitches. The tension may need to be adjusted every few stitches, as the stitching will not be as smooth if any of the strands are at all loose.

EMBROIDERY

❖

Small leaves: Using three strands of melaleuca (802) thread, stitch the small leaves first by placing a 16-wrap Bullion Stitch on each side of the central vein. This will create padding to support the alternating Satin Stitch and achieve a dimensional effect. Couch the Bullion Stitches to the fabric following the curve of the leaf and referring to diagram 1, starting at the leaf tip and working an alternating Satin Stitch. Cover the entire leaf keeping the stitches very close together and ensuring that each Bullion Stitch is well covered.

Tendrils: Thread the No 8 crewel needle with the Gold Handsew Metal Thread and work Stem Stitch from the leaf centre to create the fine wavy tendrils.

Hint: Although Sadi appears to be a coiled 'spring', do not stretch it as it will not return to its original shape. The fine smooth Sadi is very fragile and easily crushed or bent, so don't pull the thread too tightly when attaching it to your project. Also, as the Sadi has a tendency to be 'bouncy' it is recommended you hold it over a small piece of velvet when cutting it.

Roses: Thread the No 9 milliner's needle with three strands of the ecru thread and work four, double-wrap French Knots in the centre of the rose, ensuring they are close together and form a square. These French Knots are used as reference points for placing the petals.

MATERIALS

- 15cm (6in) square cream polyester shantung
- Rajmahal Art Silk Thread: one skein each of melaleuca (802), sassafras (805), ecru
- Rajmahal Smooth Sadi Gold Fine: one packet
- Rajmahal Pearl Sadi Gold Fine: one packet
- Rajmahal Shisha Glass Mirror: four small diamonds
- Fine strong beading thread
- Rajmahal Gold Handsew Metal Thread: one reel
- 10cm (4in) Framecraft jewellery bowl
- No 10 and 11 beading needles
- No 8 crewel needle
- No 9 milliner's needle
- Fine wire-cutters
- Very light, sharp pencil

STITCHES USED

Bullion Stitch, Couching, French Knot, Satin Stitch, Stem Stitch, Straight Stitch

***Diagram 1** – Working the small leaves*

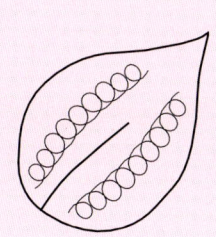

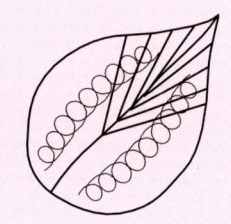

Work the Bullion Stitch then cover with an alternating Satin Stitch

Diagram 2 – *Working the small roses*

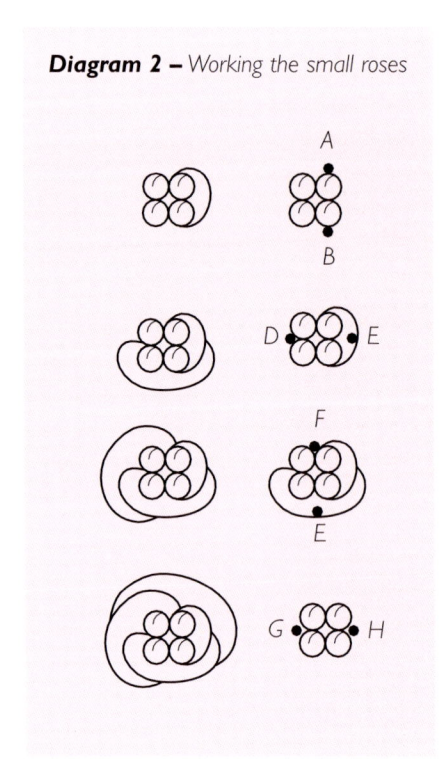

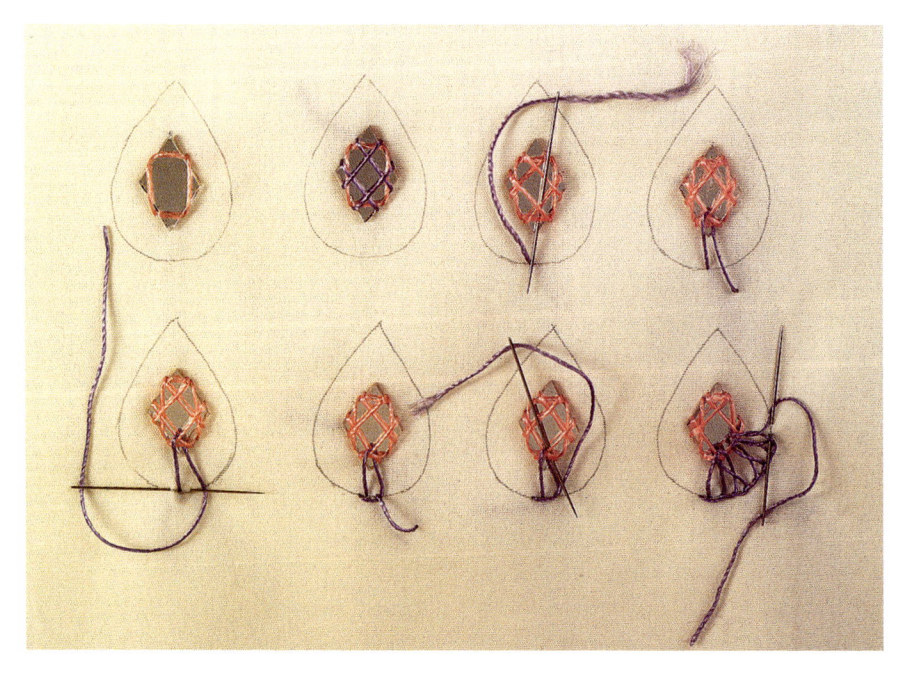

Diagram 3 – *Securing the Shisha mirrors*

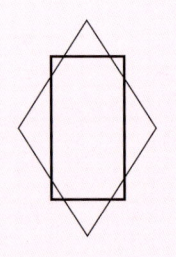

Secure the mirror by stitching across the four corners.

Work four more stitches parallel and inside the first ones.

Cut a 6mm ($1/4$in) piece of the fine smooth Sadi and thread the No 11 beading needle with a length of beading thread. Bring the needle up at point A, then thread the Sadi on to the needle and re-enter the fabric at point B, following diagram 2. Take care that the Sadi pieces curve around the French Knots, and not over the top of them. Cut another 7mm ($1/4$in) piece of the fine smooth Sadi and place it from point C to point D in the same manner as before. Placing subsequent pieces underneath previous ones hides the ends and raises the rose for a more dimensional effect. Continue to follow diagram 2 and to cut each piece approximately 1mm ($1/16$in) longer than the previous one until you reach 12mm ($1/2$in). Notice that each newly added piece starts halfway back into the previous piece. The rose will be the required size when it covers slightly more than the base of the small leaves. When the final piece of Sadi has been added it should curve around the rose, and both ends should be tucked up under a previous piece. Depending on the stitching, the French Knots that were placed in the centre of the rose may not be visible once the petals are completed.

Shisha leaves: Thread the No 8 crewel needle with three strands of sassafras (805) thread. Shisha mirrors are initially secured to the fabric by a series of Straight Stitches. Follow diagram 3 and work the first set of Straight Stitches across the four corners, then place an additional four Straight Stitches parallel to the edges. The leaves are ornamented with one of numerous stitches used to embellish and secure the Shisha mirrors. This particular Shisha Stitch, in diagram 4, is a variation of Twisted Blanket Stitch. Bring your thread up at the base of the leaf at point A, then take the needle and thread under the Straight Stitches and pull them through. Take the needle down through the fabric at point B and back up at point C, making sure that these two points are very close together. Take the needle and thread under the Straight Stitches again, making sure the needle goes over the sewing thread, pierce the fabric at point D and emerge at point E. It is essential that point D is inside the loop created by the previous stitch and the sewing thread is looped under your needle. Continue in this manner, looping each stitch through the Straight Stitches and then securing them to the fabric.

When working the stitches through the fabric, be sure that you are following the outline of the leaf.

At the leaf tip take a small Straight Stitch to secure your loop then, following diagram 5, emerge at point A inside the loop and continue the stitch. This will give the leaf a more definite point. Continue working the stitches until you have completed the leaf.

Centre flower: This flower is fashioned after the Japanese violet that is traditionally worked in Brazilian embroidery and is begun on a small circle marked with five points, refer to diagram 6. Cut 10 pieces of Pearl Sadi, each 28mm (1 1/8in) long, pre-bending them around a round pencil (not hexagonal) and making sure you don't stretch or kink them. Thread the No 10 beading needle

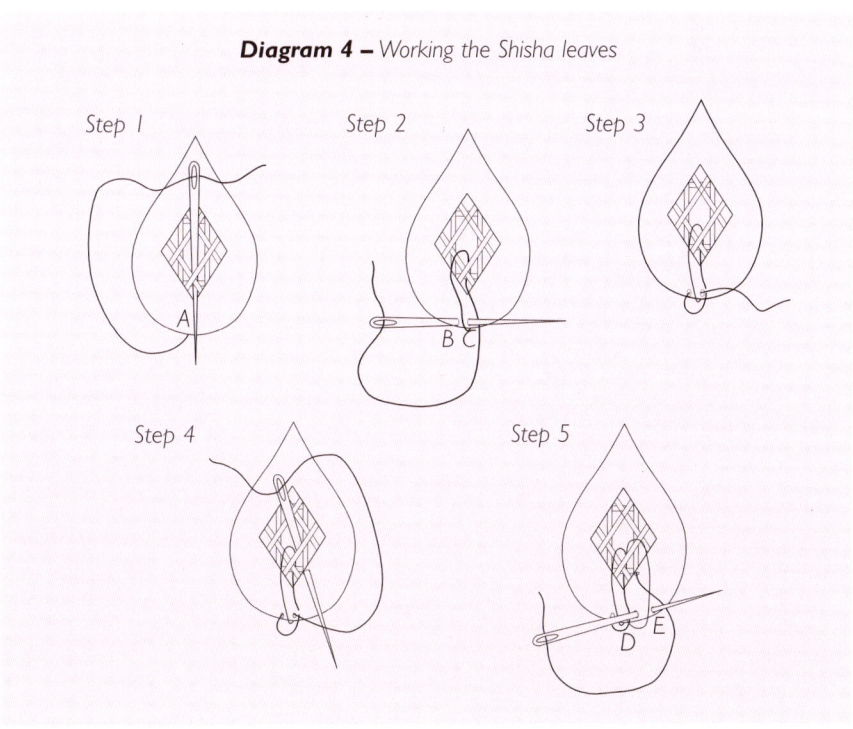

Diagram 4 – *Working the Shisha leaves*

Step 1 *Step 2* *Step 3*

Step 4 *Step 5*

EMBROIDERY TREASURES

Diagram 5 – *Shisha leaf tip*

Diagram 6 – *Stitching the centre flower*

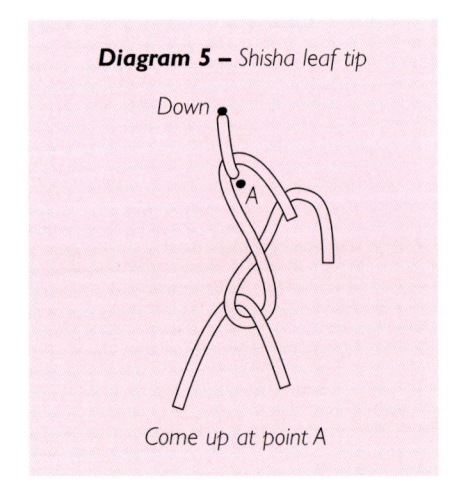

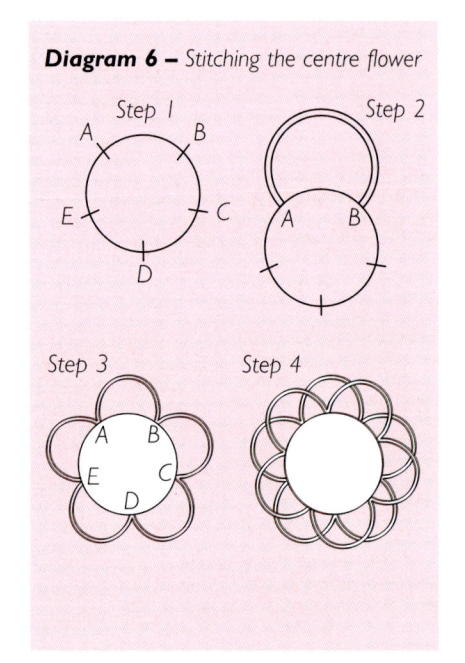

with the beading thread and emerge at point A, on diagram 6. Slide the needle all the way through the hollow centre of one piece of the Pearl Sadi, before taking the needle and beading thread only to the back of the fabric at point B. Couch the coil down at each end, placing the Couching Stitch between the first two or three coils only. If you Couch too far up the coil, your flower will be very stiff and flat. Continue to place petals in this manner around the circle, then repeat the previous steps at the five points between the previous stitches. This second row of petals will lie on top of the first row completed.

To finish off, thread a No 9 milliner's needle with three strands of ecru thread and fill the centre of the flower with three-wrap French Knots.

FINISHING

❖

Your exquisite embroidery is now ready to be placed on the lid of the jewellery bowl following the manufacturer's instructions. ✯

EMBROIDERY TREASURES *Diamonds and Roses*

'Happy Birthday' Cake Band

Birthdays are always a special time, so why not add to the festive mood by lighting some candles on the birthday cake in this fun cross-stitched band by Sarah Ricketts.

PREPARATION

❖

This design was created to fit a 19cm (7¹/2in) diameter cake. It can be made larger by repeating the candle motifs to the length required and it is secured by velcro fastening stitched underneath the candle motifs.

EMBROIDERY

❖

As the Aida band is pre-edged, there is no need to overlock or hand-sew the edges. Fold the band in half to find the centre. Find the centre of the graph, following the arrows from the sides and begin stitching the design from the centre. Using a hoop or lap frame is not recommended when working with Aida bands.

The embroidery cotton should be separated into six strands and then put together to thread the needle. This helps to eliminate knots while stitching. When using two strands, do not thread them separately through the needle at once, instead, the 'loop method' should be used. A single strand of thread is doubled over and then the two ends thread through the needle together. Push the needle into the fabric from the front to the back. Bring the needle up through the hole diagonally opposite to form half a stitch. Pass the needle through the loop of thread and draw the stitch so created to the back of the work. This is the neatest and most economical way of starting to stitch and it is also the easiest, especially when working on small individual areas, such as some of the shadows. However, although it can be used when working with odd numbers of threads, it is a great deal easier when using an even number.

Make one full Cross Stitch, using two strands of thread, for every square on the graph containing a symbol. You may stitch from left to right or vice versa, whichever is more comfortable. It is important that the top stitch in each row is executed in the same direction for the whole of the piece.

To finish off a thread, bring it to the back of the work and run it under five to 10 stitches to anchor it. Snip off the excess thread close to the work.

Each candle is outlined in Back Stitch in the same colour as the candle, using two strands of thread.

FINISHING

❖

To make up the band, start at the right-hand side of the band, fold the fabric underneath two holes along from the last candle. Tack this edge with the white sewing-machine thread, ensuring that the tricot edging is folded in half so that both edges match. Stitch the 'hook' side of the velcro into place in the turned-under fabric. Trim the band approximately 10 holes away from the end of the velcro, turn under and tack. Pin through the fabric and tack both sides together. On the left hand side of

MATERIALS

- DMC Stranded Embroidery Cotton: one skein each of medium yellow (743), peacock blue (807), very dark coral red (817), forest green (989), very light antique blue (3752)
- 4.5cm (1³/4in) Zweigart Aida Band: 80cm (31¹/2in) red-edged
- No 24 or No 26 tapestry needle
- Sewing-machine thread: one reel of white
- 7cm (2³/4in) velcro

DESIGN SIZE

3cm x 59.5cm (1¹/4in x 23³/4in)

STITCHES USED

Back Stitch, Cross Stitch

EMBROIDERY TREASURES

the band, place the other half of the velcro six holes away from the last candle and stitch it into place. Fold the fabric underneath and complete as for the right-hand side.

For further information, contact Sarah L. Ricketts on (03) 9809 4889 or email her at sarah@sarah.com.au ✯

Happy Easter Bookmark and Greeting Card

Vivienne Garforth has created two versions of the same design. The bookmark has wording and a lily – perfect for a male – while a feminine touch is added to the greeting card with the a wreath of roses.

MATERIALS

- 18cm x 22cm (7¹/8in x 8³/4in) 25-count white or ivory Lugano cloth
- Rajmahal Art Silk Thread: one strand of ecru, cream, tangier sand (44), white (96), imperial purple (115), persimmon (144), woodlands brown (171), barely pink (200), petal pink (202), green earth (421), maidenhair green (521)
- Rajmahal Metal Hand Sewing Thread: one reel of gold
- DMC Perlé No 8 Thread: one ball of white
- 30cm x 3mm (12in x ¹/8in) white satin ribbon for the bookmark
- No 24 tapestry needle
- No 9 crewel needle
- White or ivory blank card with a rectangular aperture of 13cm x 10cm (5¹/8in x 4in)
- Small, sharp scissors
- 15cm (6in) embroidery hoop (optional)
- Craft glue

DESIGN SIZE

11cm x 7.5cm (4³/8in x 3in)

STITCHES USED

Back Stitch, Blanket Stitch, Cross Stitch, Kloster Blocks, Satin Stitch

PREPARATION

Run a tacking thread across the centre of the fabric, both vertically and horizontally to find the central point. The No 24 tapestry needle is used for the Hardanger embroidery while the No 9 crewel needle is used for all other embroidery.

EMBROIDERY

Using one strand of silk thread over two fabric threads, begin Cross-stitching from the intersection of the two tacking threads. Once the Cross-stitching has been completed, Back-stitch around the letters with the gold metal thread, maidenhair green (521) around the lily and woodlands brown (171) for the veins on the leaf.

By working the Cross-stitching first, it will be easier to follow the diagram for the Hardanger as it will provide reference points. Work the outside edges first using white Perlé No 8 thread. For the bookmark, work Blanket Stitch over four fabric threads, but for the card work Satin Stitch, also over four fabric threads. The Blanket Stitch will provide a firm edge for the bookmark once the cross has been cut from the fabric.

The Kloster Blocks are worked using five Satin Stitches over four fabric threads, making sure that each block corresponds in position with the ones above, below and on both sides. This is imperative when it comes to cutting fabric threads.

Finally, fill in all the cut holes with a simple lace filling stitch. Weave the needle through the back of the sewn blocks, leaving a tail of 1.5mm ($^1/_{16}$in). Over-sew around the back of one of the stitches to secure the tail and then bring the needle up to the left of the central stitch of a block of Satin Stitches. Slip the needle under the central stitch in the Satin-stitch block on the right, from top to bottom and coming up by the previous thread. Continue around the cut-out square, making sure that the thread is not pulled too tightly and going down underneath and to the right of the starting loop.

FINISHING

❖

Carefully cut around the edge of the bookmark, making sure you don't cut any of the stitches. For the bookmark, insert the ribbon through the bottom central Hardanger square and tie a knot at the back of the work to secure it. For the card, simply cut a rectangle with a seam of 1.5cm ($^5/_8$in) larger than the aperture of the card. Spread a thin line of glue around the aperture and place the card, right side up over the embroidery. Turn the front of the card over the centre section and add a thin line of glue around the edge to secure it firmly in place. ★

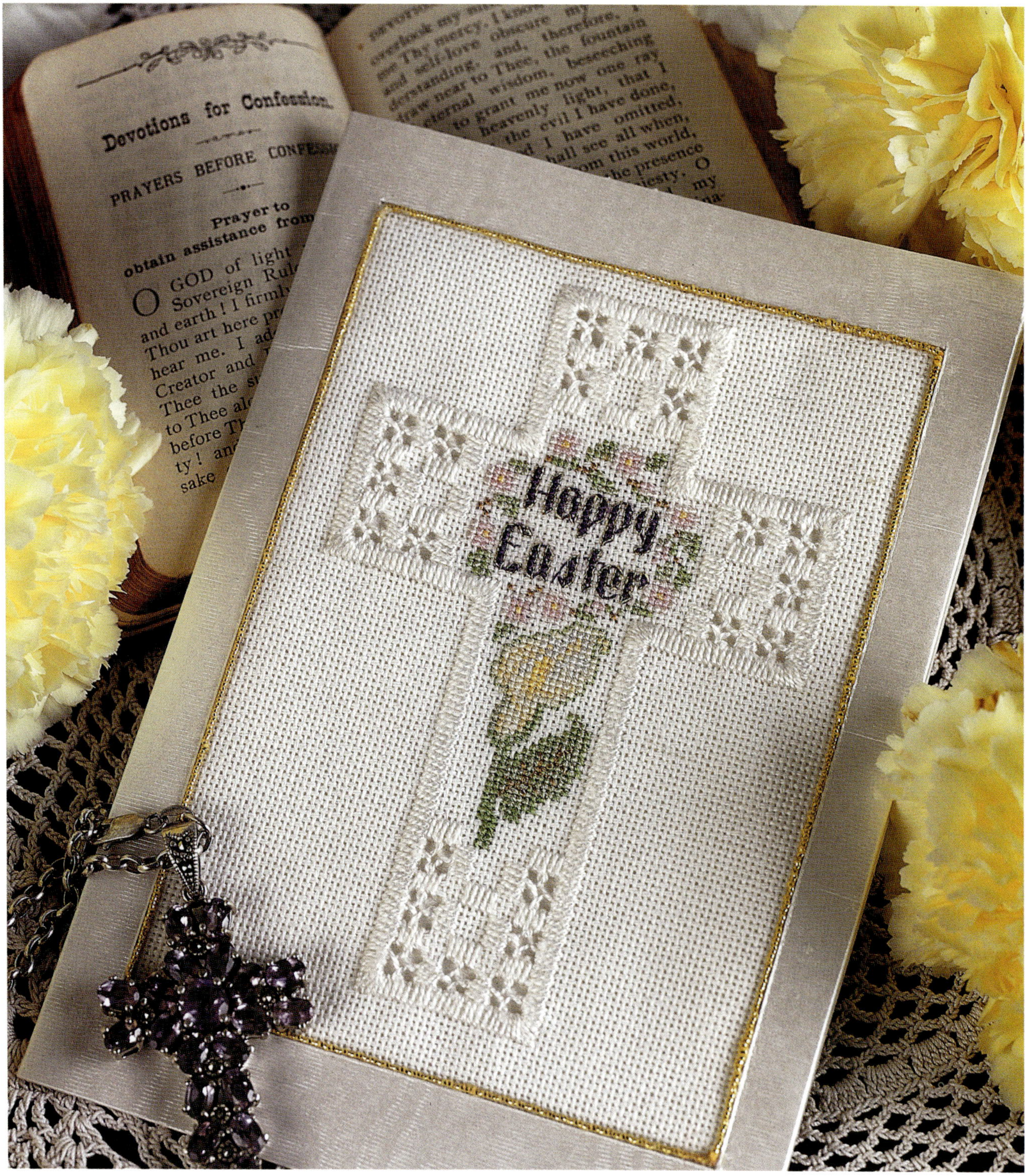
Devotions for Confession.
Happy Easter

Pastel Blossoms

Rosemarie Hanauer has combined the luxurious sheen of rayon threads beautifully with pastel matt wools to create a delicate wreath of blooms, evoking an image of peace and harmony.

MATERIALS

- 35cm (13¾in) square piece of doctor flannel
- 35cm x 45cm (13¾in x 18in) cream fabric for the cushion back
- Edmar Iris Rayon Thread: one skein each of pale apricot (168), pale sea green (227)
- Gumnut Perlé Silk Jewels: one skein of topaz light
- Gumnut Opals Thread: one skein of turquoise light
- Gumnut Crewel Wool Blossoms: one skein of (621)
- Kacoonda Thick Silk Thread: one packet of ecru (4)
- Marlitt Rayon Thread: one skein of pale gold (1012)
- Paterna Wool: one skein of cream (262)
- YLI Candlelight Metallic Yarn: one spool of Rainbow (RNB)
- YLI Stranded Silk Floss: one packet of (166)
- Delica Beads: one packet of DBR 35
- Mill Hill Glass Seed Beads: one packet of cream (00123)
- No 18 and 22 chenille needles
- No 7 crewel needle
- No 1 and 8 milliner's needles
- Cream sewing-machine thread
- 35cm (13¾in) cream zipper
- 35cm (13¾in) pillow insert
- Water-soluble marking pen

DESIGN SIZE

35cm (13¾in)

STITCHES USED

Bullion Lazy Daisy Stitch, Colonial Knot, Fly Stitch, French Knot, Granitos Stitch, Lazy Daisy Stitch, Pistil Stitch, Stem Stitch, Straight Stitch, Twisted Fly Stitch.

PREPARATION

Ensuring that the design is centred, transfer the outline from the centre pattern sheet onto the doctor flannel with the water-soluble marking pen. Carefully remove the pen markings as you embroider each section of the design.

EMBROIDERY

The chenille needles are used with the thicker threads and wools and the crewel needle for the finer silks and rayon threads. Stitch the large daisies using the No 1 milliner's needle and attach the beads with the No 8 milliner's needle. This will have an eye small enough to slide through the beads and be easier to handle than a beading needle.

Blossoms: Using one strand of cream (262) wool, work each petal as a five-stitch Granitos. The outer tip of the petal has a Fly Stitch in ecru (4) thick silk and a small Straight Stitch in the same thread. Stitch all five petals of each blossom in the same way before filling the centre with cream beads attached with the cream sewing-machine thread.

Blossom buds: Using one strand of cream (262) and one strand of ecru (4) silk in the same needle, work each bud as a four-stitch Granitos.

Blossom stems and leaves: These are stitched in one strand of (621) crewel wool. Begin with the stem worked in Stem Stitch then work the leaves by stacking Fly Stitches to fill the shape. Start the leaves at their tip and move down each one finishing with a Pistil Stitch with the knot at the base of the leaf. Try to create curved veins in some of the leaves to add realism and variety to your embroidery. Complete the bud with a Twisted Fly Stitch and four or five Straight Stitches to give the illusion of sepals and calyx.

Forget-me-nots: Stitch the forget-me-nots near the blossoms with five Colonial Knots in one strand of turquoise light, and a French Knot in the centre in four strands of pale gold (1012) rayon. Lazy Daisy-stitch the leaves in three strands of (166) thread and scatter them around the flowers.

Bead flower spray and Queen Anne's lace: Sprays of DBR (35) are attached with the cream sewing-machine thread in the positions indicated on the design outline. Stem-stitch the stems of the Queen Anne's lace in topaz light, then work a French Knot followed by four or five Straight Stitches to form a fan. The tiny flowers at the end are French Knots in one strand of Rainbow metallic thread. Create large and small flower heads around your embroidery by varying the number of French Knots used.

Daisy: Following diagram 1, draw two concentric circles at the position for each daisy and fill the outer area with Bullion Lazy Daisy Stitches in pale apricot (168), before working French Knots in two strands of pale gold (1012) to cover the centre. The buds are worked as three Bullion Lazy Daisy Stitches in pale apricot (168) surrounded by a Twisted Fly Stitch with a long tail, anchored near the main flower. The delicate leaves are worked in alternating Satin Stitch in pale sea green (227), and are attached to the main flower with a Pistil Stitch having the knot end at the leaf.

Remaining forget-me-nots: These flowers, near the Queen Anne's lace and daisies, are stitched in the same manner as the previous ones but with five French Knots to complete them and only two strands of pale gold (1012) rayon thread

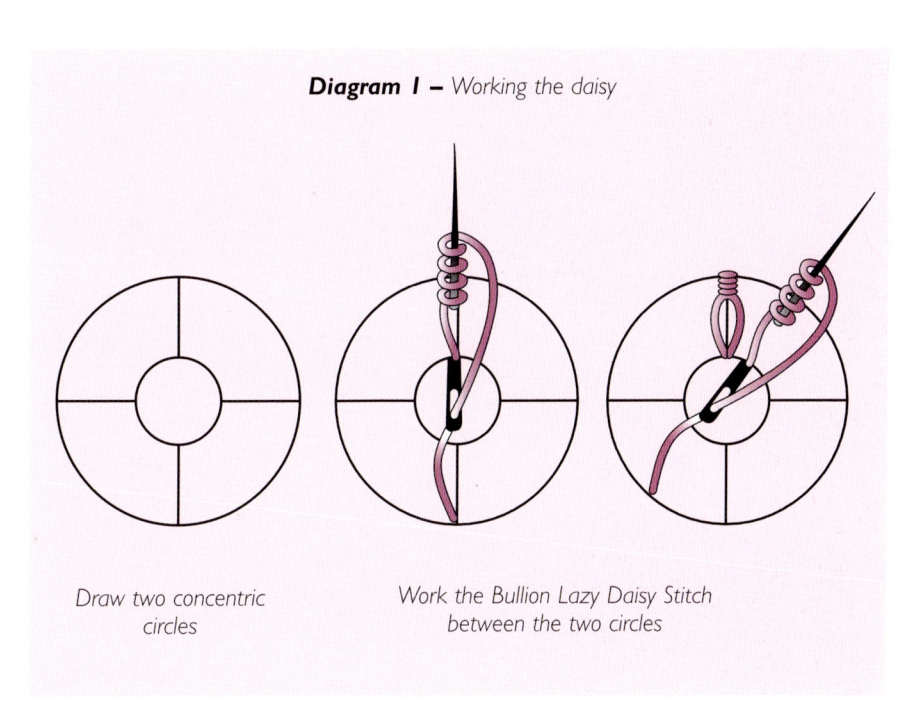

***Diagram 1** – Working the daisy*

Draw two concentric circles

Work the Bullion Lazy Daisy Stitch between the two circles

for the French Knot in the centre. The leaves are also smaller and worked in two strands of (166) thread as Lazy Daisy Stitches.

FINISHING

❖

Remove any remaining marking outlines and round off the corners of the doctor flannel embroidered cushion front. Stitch the zip to one edge of the cream cushion back fabric, then stitch the back to the embroidered front, making sure the zip is left open for turning right side out. The cord is made from three sets of mixed threads to create one larger twisted cord. The first set is made of three lengths of one strand of cream (262), each 1.7m (1^7/$_8$yds) in length. The second set is one length of ecru (4) silk and two lengths of cream (262), each 1.7m (1^7/$_8$yd) long, while the third set comprises three pieces of Rainbow metallic thread 2m (2^1/$_4$yd) long and two pieces of cream (262), 1.7m (1^7/$_8$yd) in length. The metallic thread is deliberately made longer as it seems to pull up more when twisted.

Take the first set, fold each thread in half and attach it to a cup hook or door handle. Individually twist each of the doubled threads about 100 times in a clockwise direction, then put all three together and twist them in an anticlockwise direction until combined. Knot them together to ensure they do not untwist. Repeat this for the other two sets of threads to produce a total of three cords. Attach these three cords to the cup hook or door handle and twist each one individually in an anticlockwise direction about 20 times, before joining them together and allowing them to twist in a clockwise direction to combine into one large cord. Knot the ends to prevent them unravelling. When the cord is finished, slip-stitch it to the outer edges of the cushion with the cream sewing-machine thread. The two ends of the cord can be secured by being caught in the seam near the end of the zip.

For further information, contact Christina's Craft and Gifts, 208 Prospect Rd, Prospect SA 5082. Phone (08) 8344 5066 or email ccg@arcom.com.au ✶

Busy Bee Chatelaine

For the busy bees out there, Jennifer Bennett has designed a divine chatelaine and matching scissor keeper so that you can keep your accessories in mint condition when taking a break from stitching.

MATERIALS

- 75cm x 15cm (29 1/2in x 6in) natural linen
- 75cm x 15cm (29 1/2in x 6in) cream homespun
- 2, 6cm x 14cm (2 1/8in x 5 1/2in) doctor flannel
- Pellon
- YLI 9mm (3/8in) Organdie ribbon: 40cm (16in) of 56
- Madeira Glissen Gloss Metallic Flash: one reel of 03
- Anchor Stranded Cotton: one skein each of 403, 307
- DMC Perlé No 5 Thread: one skein of black
- Mill Hill Glass Seed Beads: one packet of black (02014)
- No 10 embroidery needle
- No 13 and 20 chenille needle
- Templastic
- 10cm (4in) embroidery hoop
- Pigma pen
- Tracing paper
- Pencil
- Dental floss or linen thread
- Double-sided tape or glue
- Eyebrow brush

DESIGN SIZE

Bee: 3cm (1 1/4in) square

Needlebook: 7cm x 8cm (2 3/4in x 3 1/4in)

Scabbard: 11cm x 5cm (4 3/8in x 2in)

Tassel: 4cm (1 1/2in) square

STITCHES USED

Back Stitch,
Fly Stitch,
Palestrina Knots,
Ribbon Stitch,
Straight Stitch,
Turkey Stitch

PREPARATION

Using your preferred light source, trace all the areas for stitching and embroidery from the pattern sheet onto the natural linen fabric. Mount the homespun under the natural linen fabric and tack to hold it in place. Tack around the outlines of the scabbard, tassel and needlebook. Trace the embroidered areas and mark them with the pigma pen on the moiré fabric. To embroider each area, mount them into the 10cm (4in) embroidery hoop.

EMBROIDERY

Bee: The bee is worked in the same manner for all the chatelaine pieces and you can refer to the pattern sheet for its placement. Take a length of black No 5 Perlé thread and tack around the edge of the bee and its markings. Change to two strands and commence filling in the rear end of the bee with Turkey Stitches. Refer to diagram 1. Once this area has been filled, change to the brown cotton and Turkey-stitch the next band. Alternate the bands until the body has been completed. Next, trim the knots and brush with an eyebrow brush. Trim any uneven areas. Ribbon-stitch the wings using the 9mm (3/8in) organdie (56) ribbon, then mark the veins on the wings with Fly Stitch and one strand of (03) metallic flash thread. In the same thread, Back-stitch the legs. Using one strand of the black cotton, securely attach two black seed beads for the bee's eyes.

FINISHING

Cushion: Cut out the cushion along the marked lines. Place right side up, fold right and left sides along fold lines, then fold to meet in the centre. Pin to hold.

Diagram 1 – *Turkey Stitch*

This stitch is a pile stitch, which makes a series of closely worked loops. These are cut and trimmed after the stitching is finished to give a pile similar to that of a carpet. The loops should be worked round a pencil or large knitting needle to keep the size constant. Each loop is secured by a Back Stitch as shown. Each row is worked above the preceding row, keeping the rows as close together as possible.

Machine-stitch along top and bottom lines. Trim the corners and turn right side out.

Cord: Take a length of 40cm (16in) of black No 5 Perlé thread to make a cord. Fold the strands in half and tie a knot at one end of the cord. You can pin this onto an ironing board, hook or door handle. Twist the cord tightly until it starts to kink, slip the cord off where it is secured and fold in half again. Let go of the folded ended so that the cord twists back on itself. Knot the ends and place cord through the No 13 chenille needle. Pull from an inside corner of the cushion.

Tassel: Refer to diagram 2 for making the tassel.

Thread the No 13 chenille needle and slip the needle through the head of the tassel, Buttonhole Stitch over the top of the band created and continue until the top of the tassel is covered.

Scissor Scabbard: Cut out the embroidered scabbard pieces, leaving a 2cm (3/4in) seam allowance. Cut the homespun close to the tacked edge. Tack close to the marked edge of the scabbard pieces using strong thread or dental floss. Do not knot or end off this thread and leave sufficient tails to pull tight. From the templastic, cut one of the front and two of the back scabbard pieces. Place double-sided tape or glue on one side of the plastic scabbard front. Place the front glued side down onto the Pellon, press firmly to hold it and cut the Pellon to fit. Place another layer of tape or glue on the other side of the scabbard, carefully place the Pellon side against the homespun side of the embroidery, and pull the threads tightly to fit around the templastic. Finger-press the raw edges onto the glue to hold it.

Repeat the process for the scabbard back and linings.

Place the back and back lining pieces together making sure the top edges match, and work a row of Palestrina Knots around the edge, catching both pieces when stitching between the marked area. Refer to diagram 3. Use one strand of black No 5 Perlé thread. Repeat the process for the front scabbard pieces. Lay both front and back shapes together and continue to stitch Palestrina Knots around the lower edge of the scabbard, catching both the front and back pieces together to join them.

Needlebook: Cut out the needlebook area leaving a seam allowance of 2cm (3/4in).

Diagram 2 – *Making a Tassel*

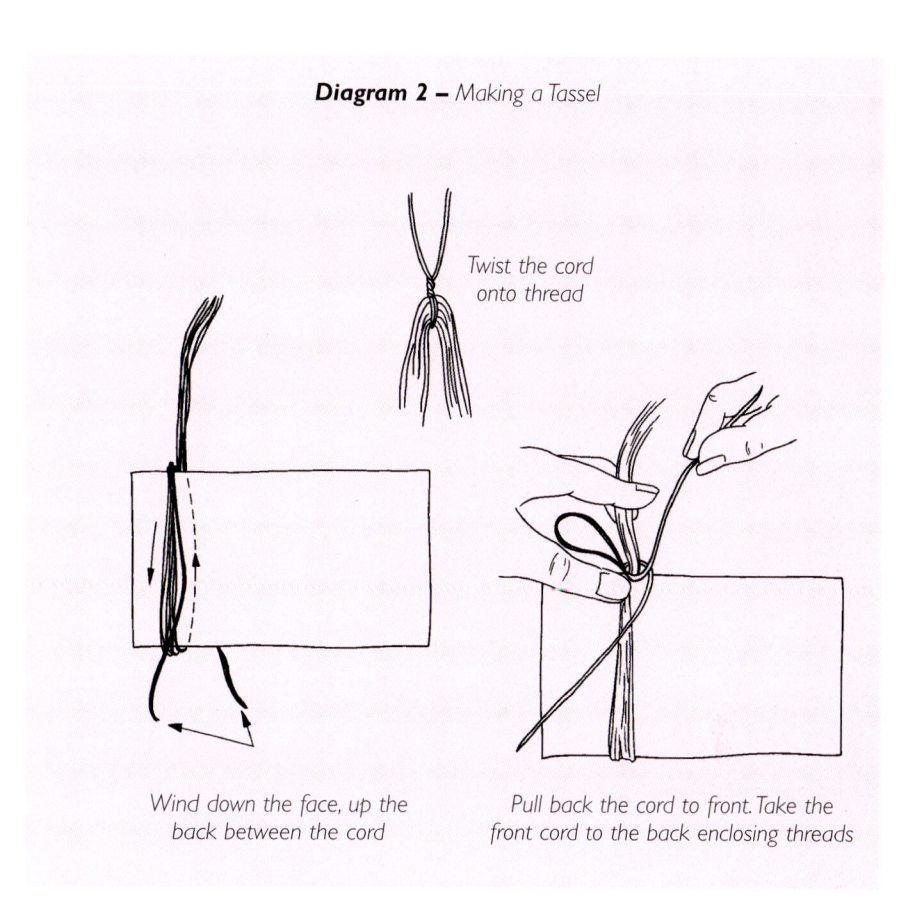

Twist the cord onto thread

Wind down the face, up the back between the cord

Pull back the cord to front. Take the front cord to the back enclosing threads

Diagram 3 – *Palestrina Knot Stitch*

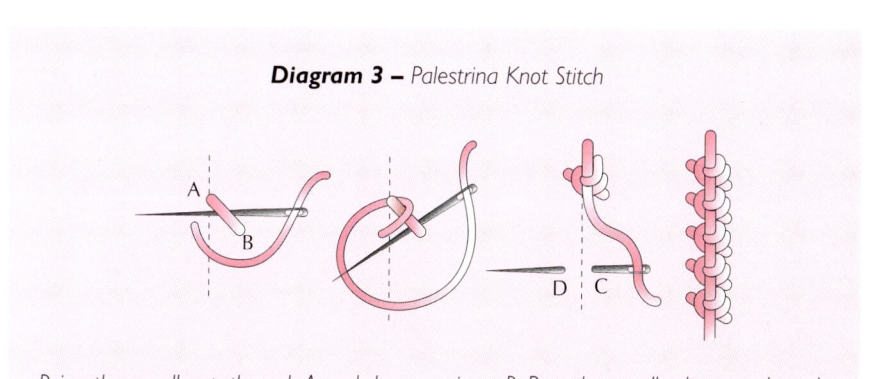

Bring the needle up through A and down again at B. Pass the needle downwards under the surface stitch just made without piercing the fabric. With the thread under the needle, pass the needle again under the first stitch. Pull the thread through to form a knot. The knots should be spaced evenly and closely to have a beaded effect.

Machine-stitch around the marked lines of the needlebook in a sewing-machine thread to match the natural linen fabric. Place the needlebook right side up, fold the left-hand lining along a narrow fold line, and fold the right-hand lining also along the narrow fold line. Then fold both sides along the stitch line at the edge of the needlebook. Both edges should meet in the centre. Pin them to hold and stitch across the top and bottom of the needlebook. Trim the corners and turn to the right side. Cut two rectangular shapes from the templastic. Add double-sided tape or glue to both sides of the templastic rectangles. These fit into the back and front of the needlebook to form a firm cover, add the Pellon to fit then slide the shapes into each side of the needlebook – they may need to be trimmed. Slip-stitch them together and insert the doctor flannel pages.

Stitch Palestrina Knots around the edge of the needlebook using one strand of black Perlé thread.

For further information, contact Jennifer Bee, 395 Raymond St, Sale Vic 3850. Phone/fax (03) 5143 2899 or email jenniferbee395@hotmail.com ✯

Ring of Roses

*Talented embroiderer, Wendie Young, has created this gorgeous
'ring of roses' in tones of pink and green on cream linen –
the perfect addition to your wall of favourites.*

EMBROIDERY TREASURES

MATERIALS

- 28cm (11in) square crewel linen
- Kacoonda 4mm ($1/8$in) Silk Ribbon: 50cm (20in) of green (8E)
- Kacoonda 7mm ($1/4$in) Silk Ribbon: 3m ($3 1/4$yds) of antique (101); 2.5m ($2 3/4$yds) of green (8E)
- Kacoonda Fine Silk Thread: one packet of green (8E)
- No 18 chenille needle
- No 8 crewel needle
- 18cm ($7 1/8$in) embroidery hoop
- Sharp, soft lead pencil

DESIGN SIZE

12cm ($4 3/4$in) square

STITCHES USED

Double Side Ribbon Stitch, Ribbon Stitch, Side Ribbon Stitch, Stem Stitch, Straight Stitch, Twirled Straight Stitch

***Diagram 1** – Rose petal placement*

***Diagram 2** – Rosebuds*

HINTS FOR WORKING WITH RIBBONS

❖

To help prevent damage to your silk ribbon, use only short lengths of approximately 30-38cm (12-15in). Using the large chenille needle will help open the weave of the fabric, enabling the ribbon to pass through more easily. After threading the needle, knot the end of the ribbon. When finishing off, do not pass the needle back and forth, or try to knot the ribbon. Simply cut it leaving a 1cm ($3/8$in) tail, then stitch it down with a thread to match your fabric.

PREPARATION

❖

Centre your linen over the design outline on the pattern sheet and using your preferred light source and a very sharp pencil, trace the pattern onto the linen. Place the traced linen in the embroidery hoop.

EMBROIDERY

❖

Rose vine: Using three strands of green (8E) fine silk thread in the No 8 crewel needle and following the traced pattern lines, stitch the vine in Stem Stitch with the thread held up.

Roses: The two full-blown roses are stitched using a No 18 chenille needle and the antique (101) silk ribbon. From the wrong side of the linen bring the needle out in the centre at the base of the rose and work one loose Ribbon Stitch. Work a Side Ribbon Stitch on each side of the first Ribbon Stitch, referring to diagram 1 for the rose petal placement and ensuring these petals roll away from the centre. Working from side to side, add more petals to form a semicircle fanning out from the centre. Make sure you shorten the length of each subsequent petal or you will have a daisy instead of a rose! Continue stitching around your top-heavy circle, stitching the base of three or four petals in Ribbon Stitch. To complete the rose, stitch three or four Ribbon Stitches from the central spot fanning out across the front and through the back petals. Lift these front petals with the eye of the needle so they do not lie flat.

Rosebuds: The buds are formed in a similar manner to the first five or seven petals on the rose but are packed closely together. Thread a No 18 chenille needle with the antique (101) silk ribbon and stitch the central Ribbon Stitch. Add one or two Side Ribbon Stitches on each side depending on the finished size of the bud you require, following diagram 2.

Using the 7mm ($1/4$in) green (8E) silk ribbon, make a Side Ribbon Stitch on either side of the bud to form the sepals. To complete the bud, work a Straight Stitch across the base to form the calyx.

Stems: These are worked using the 4mm ($1/8$in) green (8E) silk ribbon in a No 18 chenille needle using Twirled Straight Stitch. Bring the needle out at the base of the stem, twirl the needle to spiral the ribbon. Pull tight on the ribbon, then pull the stitch down into the base of the flower or bud.

Leaves: Refer to the illustration and photograph as your guide to the size and style of each leaf. Use the 7mm ($1/4$in) green (8E) silk ribbon in the No 18 chenille needle and work the leaves using a combination of Double Side Ribbon Stitch, Ribbon Stitch, and Side Ribbon Stitch.

EMBROIDERY TREASURES

Ring of Roses

Embroidery design

FINISHING

❖

Iron the background fabric, carefully avoiding your ribbon work. Your work is now ready to be professionally framed.

For further information, contact Treasures by Wendie, PO Box 7192, Karingal Centre Vic 3199, phone (03) 9775 7849. ✯

Cherry Pink Placemat

Dine in an air of sophistication with these stunning pink placemats designed by Linda Gryllis. Combine them with your best silverware and antique china to take full advantage of their elegance.

MATERIALS

- 34cm x 44cm (13½in x 17½in) 22-count evenweave fabric
- DMC Stranded Embroidery Cottons: two skeins of very light sportsman flesh (951); one skein of light shell pink (223) for the cherry pink placemat

  or

- three skeins of very light old gold (677); one skein of medium blue green (503) for the mint green placemat
- No 24 tapestry needle

DESIGN SIZE

Border: 36cm x 26cm (14⅜in x 10⅜in)

STITCHES USED

Back Stitch

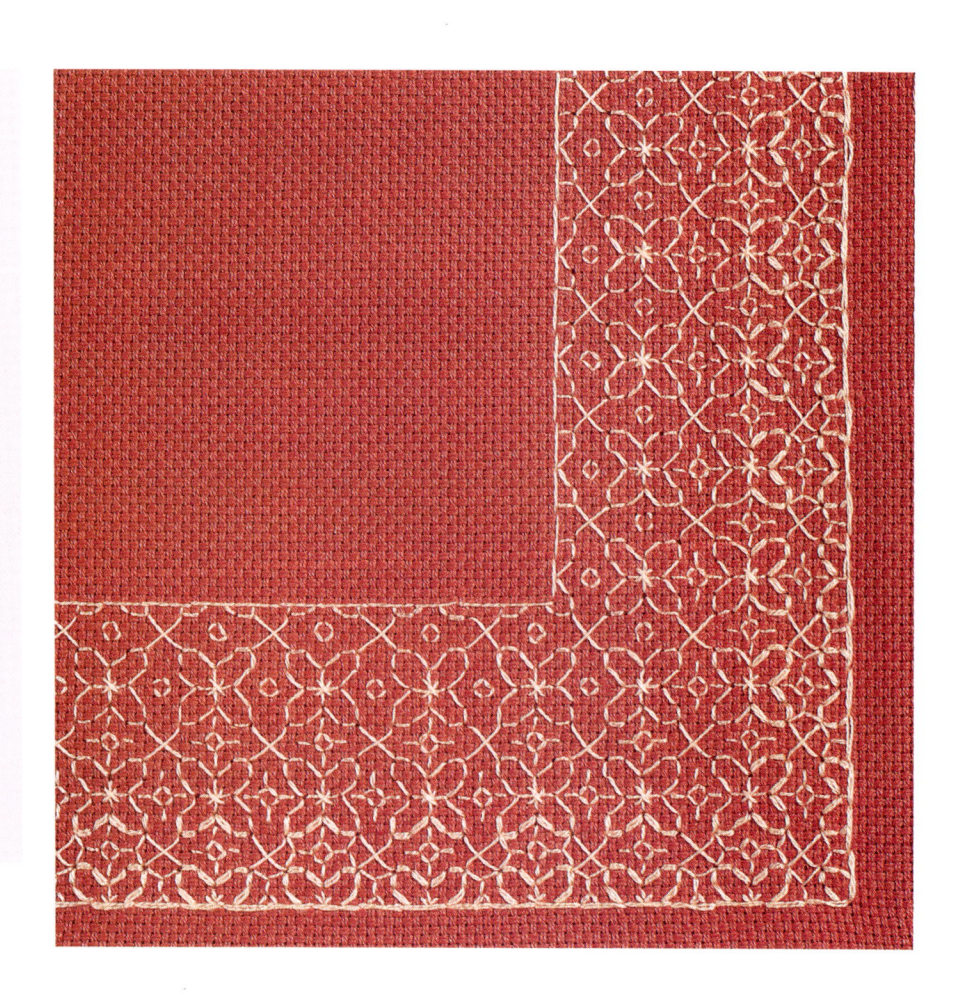

Diagram 1 – *Cherry pink placemat pattern*

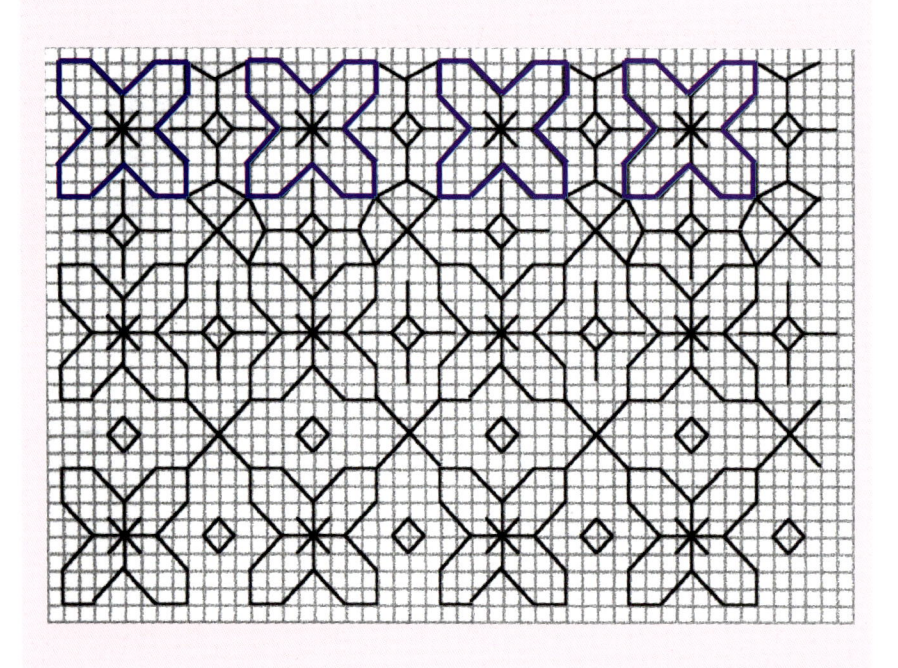

PREPARATION

❖

A cherry pink and mint green 22-count evenweave fabric was used for this project. However, you may wish to use a colour of your choice. We have provided two different blackwork designs.

Fold a 1cm (³⁄₈in) hem along one edge of the fabric and iron it. Fold it over once more and iron it down in place. Back-stitch the hem together on the line of the fabric, over five fabric threads using either the light shell pink (223) or medium blue green (503) cottons, depending on your choice of fabric. If you have chosen another colour, then match the thread to your fabric. Repeat for the three remaining sides.

EMBROIDERY

❖

Measure 1.6cm (⅝in) in from the edges of the placemat and Back-stitch over five fabric threads a rectangle border using either two strands of very light sportsman flesh (951) or very light old gold (677) embroidery cottons.

Measure 3.7cm (1⅜in) in from the first border and Back-stitching over five fabric threads, sew a rectangle using one strand of very light sportsman flesh (951) or very light old gold (677) embroidery cottons.

Begin stitching the blackwork pattern at any point within the border, with the exception of the corners. The areas marked blue in the pattern represent the use of two strands of cotton while in the black areas, one strand of cotton should be used. The stitches composed of two strands of cotton are placed towards the outside edge of the border.

The pattern will vary as you proceed around the corners. It is recommended that the top line of the pattern should be sewn first around the corner and then proceed with each line of stitching. You may need to adjust the pattern to ensure that the same proportions of double-thread stitches are used on all sides of the placemat.

Diagram 2 – *Mint green placemat pattern*

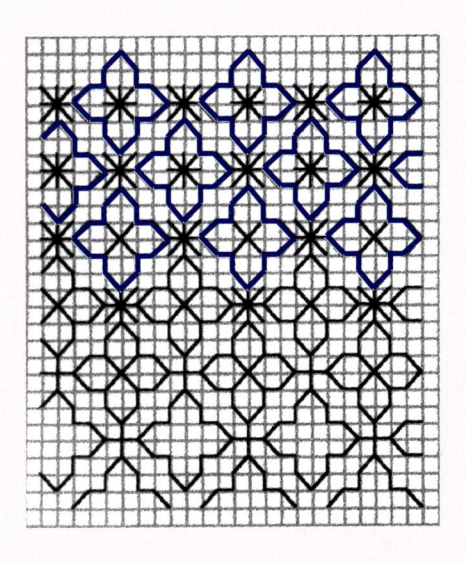

FINISHING

❖

You should find that as you come back to where you started, the pattern will begin to line up.

For further information, contact Linda Gryllis, 33 Kyre Cres, Emu Plains 2750, phone (02) 4735 3332 or visit her website at www.info-tech.com.au/lindagryllis ☆

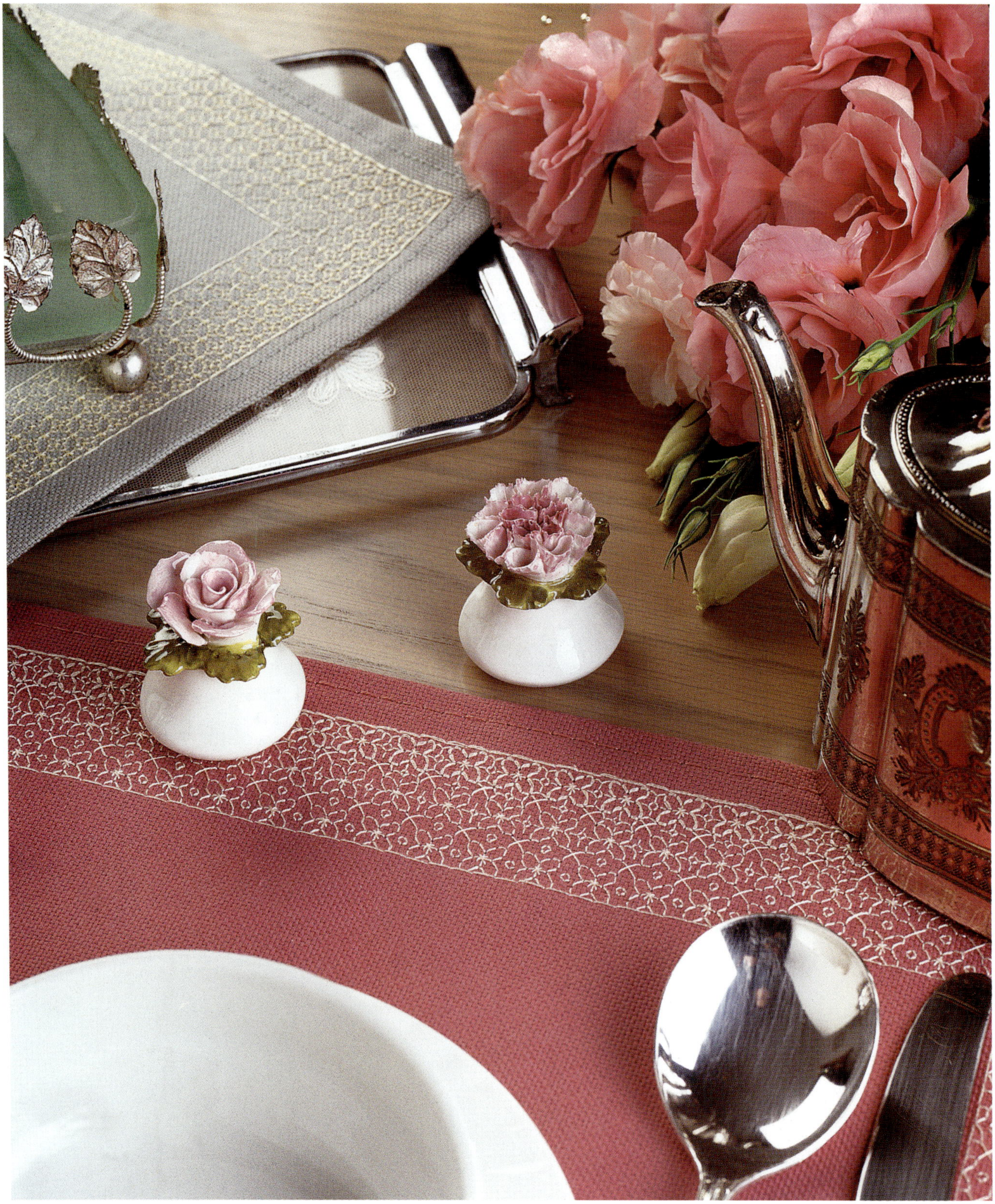

Victorian Silhouettes

Transport yourself back in time and relive the days of the elegant Victorian era with this alluring pair of traditionally dressed silhouettes designed by Maxeen Cashion.

MATERIALS

- 2, 50cm x 25cm (20in x 10in) ivory 28-count evenweave fabric
- Rajmahal Art Silk Thread: four skeins of lagerfeld ink (25)
- No 9 milliner's (straw) needle
- 25cm (10in) embroidery hoop (optional)
- Small, sharp embroidery scissors

DESIGN SIZE

Lady: 28cm x 12.5cm (11$\frac{1}{4}$in x 5in)

Gentleman: 27.5cm x 10cm (11in x 4in)

STITCHES USED

Back Stitch, Cross Stitch

PREPARATION

Overlock or hand-sew the edges of the fabric to prevent fraying. Find the fabric centre either by measuring, or by folding the fabric into quarters and marking the folds with tacking stitches. The lines will intersect at the centre of the fabric. The design chart, located on the pattern sheet, has four arrows. Draw a straight line with a ruler to intersect these arrows to give you the design centre. The centre of the fabric corresponds to the centre of the chart. Each square on the design chart represents a Cross Stitch.

EMBROIDERY

To begin, select a thread, hold the loose end behind the fabric and secure it with your first stitches. To end off the thread, run the needle through the back of several stitches to secure it. Do not use a knot in your thread as it will leave a ridge in the fabric on your finished work. Also, don't carry threads across to different areas as they can show through to the front of the fabric. Try not to pull the thread too tight but keep your tension even. Working with an embroidery hoop or lap frame helps maintain the tension better. If using an embroidery hoop, do not leave your work in the hoop when you are not working on it, as this may leave creases in the fabric that can be difficult to remove. Work the Cross Stitches and half Cross Stitches in two strands of thread. Separate the strands of the thread and allow them to untwist before combining them again to thread the needle. Begin stitching at the centre of the design. It is important that all the stitches travel in the same direction. When all the Cross-stitching is completed, work all the Back-stitching over the number of fabric threads and with the number of strands of thread as indicated in the project. Back-stitch the areas marked, following the chart.

Cross Stitch

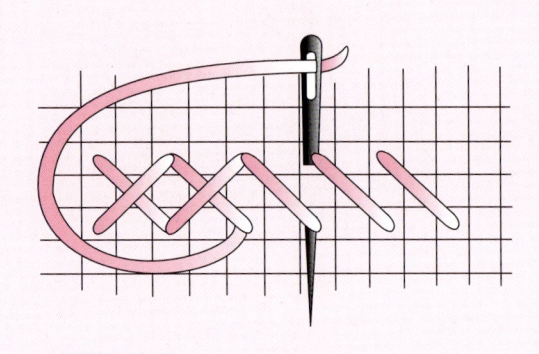

Usually worked on evenweave fabric, Cross Stitch may be worked right to left or left to right, whichever you prefer, but it is essential that all the top crosses lie in the same direction. Bring the needle up at the lower right-hand side. Take the needle up and across the same number of threads (up two and across two is the most usual). Stitch to the end of the row, forming a row of half crosses. Work back in the opposite direction, completing the crosses.

FINISHING

It is a good idea to launder your work before having it framed. Using warm water and pure soap, gently swish the fabric through the soapy water without rubbing it. Rinse it thoroughly in cold water, then gently roll it in a clean white towel to absorb any excess moisture. Do not wring the work – just lay it flat in the shade to dry. When it's dry, press the embroidery face down on a fluffy white towel with the iron on a warm setting, but don't apply pressure with the iron as this tends to flatten the stitches. ★

EMBROIDERY TREASURES *Victorian Silhouettes*

Forget-me-not Tape Measure Cover

Wendie Young has designed this exquisite tape measure cover which is certain to be a delightful addition to any keen embroiderer's sewing box.

PREPARATION

❖

Cut a 9cm (3½in) square of silk broadcloth for the front of the tape measure cover. Place the fabric over the design outline located on the pattern sheet. Using your preferred light source and the pencil, trace the embroidery design including the circle onto the fabric.

EMBROIDERY

❖

Thread the No 9 sharps needle with one strand of the (389) silk and start by Stem-stitching the lettering. To achieve a very fine look, take tiny stitches, remembering that the thread will only form straight lines, therefore it is the stitch placement that is important in achieving a curve. Never carry the thread from one letter to the next as the thread will show through to the front of your work.

Stem: Work Stem Stitches with two strands of (589) silk in the No 9 sharps needle and stitch the main stem to the point where it branches. At the branch, separate the threads and continue to stitch the remaining stem and branch with one strand only to achieve the delicate appearance.

Leaves: Refer to diagram 1 and embroider all the leaves in Satin Stitch using (589) silk in the No 9 sharps needle.

Stamens: The stamens are eyelets stitched in the centre of the forget-me-nots. Referring to diagram 2, make a small hole in the center of the flower for the eyelet using the stiletto, awl or large needle. Thread the No 9 sharps needle with one strand of (745) silk and stitch a line of small running stitches around the hole then pull the thread leaving a small tail about 1.5cm (⅝in). Work another row of tiny running stitches all around the circle, taking the last stitch through to the back and splitting the first stitch by piercing the middle of the thread. When the stitching is complete, trim the tail and reshape the hole. Bring the thread back up to the right side of the material through the middle of the eyelet, then Satin-stitch or overcast the circle by taking the thread down into the fabric just near the running stitches and coming up again in the hole. Turn your work continuously as you stitch making sure the stitches are packed together closely and you maintain a constant tension. To finish, run the thread through the back of the stitches and again reshape the eyelet if necessary.

Petals: The petals of the flowers are Granitos-stitched using (387) silk in the No 9 sharps needle. Do not start the first petal with a knot. From the front of the work scoop a tiny stitch taking only one or two strands of fabric, then pull until the end of the thread is only just visible before taking another stitch, this time making it the length of the petal. Gently pull the thread to open up the last two

MATERIALS

- 12.5cm x 19cm (5in x 7½in) cream silk broadcloth
- 7.5cm x 18cm (3in x 7⅛in) Pellon
- 7.5cm x 18cm (3in x 7⅛in) Vliesofix
- Gumnut Yarns Stranded Silk Stars: one skein each of 389, 387, 589, 745
- No 7 crewel needle
- No 9 sharps needle
- No 7 long darner needle
- Cream sewing-machine thread
- 18cm x 7.5cm (7⅛in x 3in) thick white cardboard
- 5cm (2in) diameter retractable tape measure
- Scissors
- Pencil
- Stiletto

STITCHES USED

Glove Stitch, Granitos Stitch, Satin Stitch, Stem Stitch, Whipped Chain Stitch

Diagram 1 – *Satin-stitch leaves*

Step 1   Step 2   Step 3

Diagram 2 – *Stamens or eyelets*

Step 1
Work a running stitch around the hole

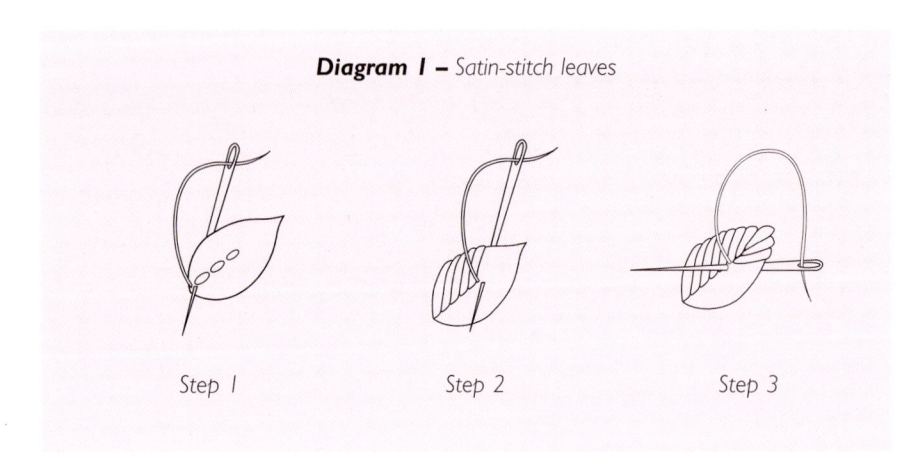

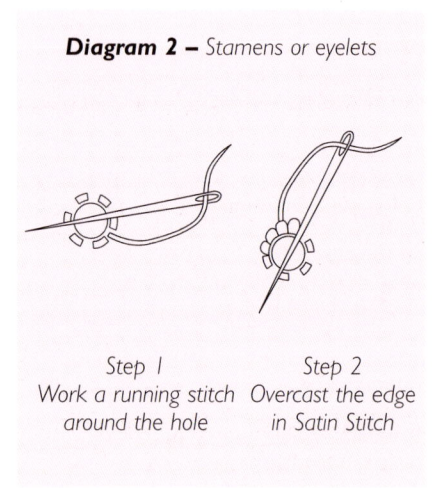

Step 2
Overcast the edge in Satin Stitch

holes stitched in the fabric. Continue stitching using these same two holes, keeping a count of the stitches used and placing the stitches from side to side rather than on top of each other until a rounded half-ball is formed. Proceed on to the next petals, taking care that they all have the same number of stitches. Having completed stitching all the petals, run the thread through to the back of the work and end it off. Press the embroidery from the back taking care not to flatten the stitches.

CONSTRUCTION

◆

Cut a 9cm (3½in) square of silk broadcloth for the back cover and using the same method as for the front, trace the circle from the pattern sheet on to the fabric. Take a length of the cream sewing-machine thread doubled and using the No 7 crewel needle, stitch a running stitch around each of the traced circles. This will be used as a gathering thread so leave a tail at both ends. Cut 5mm (¼in) around both the front and back pieces of fabric outside the traced circle.

Cut a length of silk broadcloth to 19cm x 3.5cm (7½in x 1⅜in) and one piece of Pellon, one piece of thick cardboard and two pieces of Vliesofix, all 18cm x 1.75cm (7⅛in x 1¹⁄₁₆in). From each of the Pellon, thick cardboard and the Vliesofix, cut two circles 5.5cm (2³⁄₁₆in) in diameter.

Prepare the cardboard circles by ironing the rough side of the Vliesofix to one side of each piece. When they have cooled remove the backing paper, then iron the Pellon to the Vliesofix side of the cardboard. Place the fabric circles right side down, and centre the cardboard with the Pellon side down, on top of the silk fabric. Pull the gathering thread tightly and knot off the tails, and check that the embroidery is centred over the cardboard piece.

Lace the back of each piece using a single strand of cream sewing-machine thread by taking a small stitch on the inside edge of the circle then another directly opposite. Place another stitch to the right of the first, and continue in a clockwise direction stitching from one side to the other until the whole circle is laced. These stitches should be firm but not tight. To prepare the circular wall of the cover, heat-bond the Pellon to one side of the cardboard using a piece of Vliesofix. Bond the second piece of Vliesofix to the back of the cardboard then place the prepared cardboard with the Pellon side down on top of the fabric. Fold the long sides of the fabric over to meet in the middle and iron or heat bond it to the Vliesofix before folding in the short ends and stitching them in place.

Using Glove Stitch or slip stitch and a single strand of cream sewing-machine thread, sew the top of the cover to the wall. The short ends of the wall should not meet, as this small gap is to pull the tape through.

In the same manner as the embroidered top start sewing the bottom of the cover to the other side of the wall. When you are one third of the way around, insert the tape measure into the cover making sure the button is facing the bottom and the tape is protruding out of the opening. Finish sewing the bottom of the cover in place.

Embellish the edges of the cover with a Whipped Chain Stitch using three strands of (387) silk in the No 7 long darner needle.

For further information, contact Treasures by Wendie, PO Box 7192, Karingal Centre Vic 3199, phone (03) 9775 7849. ★

Native Delights

Bring the beauty of the Australian bush indoors with this gorgeous lavender pouch designed by Joan Watters. The exquisite ribbonwork design will brighten your home whilst filling the air with the irresistible scent of fresh flowers.

PREPARATION

❖

Cut the linen into two pieces, each measuring 26cm x 16cm (10¼in x 6¼in). Cut the voile into four pieces of which three measure 26cm x 16cm (10¼in x 6¼in) for the embroidered linen bag and one is 15cm (6in) square for the flannel flower centres. Tack one of the large rectangles of voile to the wrong side of one matching piece of linen, keeping the stitches 1cm (3/8in) from the raw edge. Transfer the design outline from the pattern sheet onto the linen with the water-soluble marking pen.

EMBROIDERY

❖

Use short lengths of ribbon around 30cm (12in) long and the No 18 chenille needle, and secure the ribbon with a few stitches in the stranded cotton rather than a knot. Stitch the thread embroidery with the No 7 crewel needle.

Flannel flower: Embroider the flannel flower centres on the small square of voile which has been placed firmly in the spring hoop. Draw three small circles with a 1cm (3/8in) diameter on the voile with the water-soluble marking pen allowing plenty of space between them. Fill each circle with tightly packed Colonial Knots in three strands of light fern green (523) cotton. Remove the three embroidered centres from the voile leaving a small seam allowance around each one. Fold the seam allowance under and stitch it in place using the light fern green (523) cotton, then following the design markings, attach it to the linen with a series of Stab Stitches. Work the petals of each flannel flower in white (003) ribbon as a slightly loose Straight Stitch, then place a small Straight Stitch in one strand of white cotton in the centre of the base of each petal. Using three strands of light fern green (523), work a Fly Stitch to cup the tip of each petal, allowing the securing stitch to extend and give the petal a pointed end. Work the leaves of the flannel flower in a combination of Fly Stitch and Back Stitch, following the design outline.

Tree flower: These flowers have five even petals and a single petal for the buds. Using rose red (565) ribbon, work each petal and bud in Lazy Daisy Stitch, then with three strands of salmon (760), work a Fly Stitch to cup the tip of each petal in the same manner as the flannel flower.

In the centre of each flower, stitch three or four Colonial Knots using a combination of one strand of salmon (760) cotton and one strand of dark blue green (501) cotton in the same needle. Using the same colour mix, work a Colonial Knot at the tip of each bud. Embroider a Fly Stitch with an extended holding stitch at the base of each bud in two strands of dark blue green (501) cotton, then work the leaves beginning with a Straight Stitch and followed by a continuous Fly Stitch.

Bee: Follow diagram 1 and work the bee using three strands of the light topaz (726) cotton to embroider the Satin-stitched body. Each bee's body should be 1cm (3/8in) long and 4mm (1/8in) wide. Stitch the three stripes across the body with three strands of black (310) cotton, then work a Fly Stitch with an extended holding stitch at the tail of the bee for the sting. Work two Colonial Knots very close together to form the eyes and make two Straight Stitches in the shape of a 'V' for the antennae.

The legs are worked in Straight Stitches. Using one strand of Perlé No 5 cream (712), work two 30-wrap Bullion Stitches on each side of the bee for the wings, making sure that they overlap and curl.

MATERIALS

- 26cm x 32cm (10¼in x 12⅝in) oatmeal Belfast Linen
- 26cm x 63cm (10¼in x 24¾in) cream voile
- DMC Stranded Embroidery Cotton: one skein each of white, black (310), dark blue green (501), light fern green (523), light topaz (726), salmon (760), light brown grey (3023)
- DMC Stranded Metallic Thread: gold (5282)
- DMC Perlé No 5 Thread: one skein of cream (712)
- Bucilla 4mm (1/8in) Silk Ribbon: one card of rose red (565)
- Bucilla 7mm (1/4in) Silk Ribbon: one card of white (003)
- No 7 crewel needle
- No 18 chenille needle
- Sewing-machine thread to match the linen
- 12.5cm (5in) spring embroidery hoop
- Water-soluble marking pen
- Stiletto or knitting needle

DESIGN SIZE

Bag: 14cm x 20cm (5½in x 8in)

STITCHES USED

Back Stitch, Buttonhole Stitch, Colonial Knot, Fly Stitch, Lazy Daisy Stitch, Stab Stitch

Diagram 1 – Bee

Step 1
Bee's body

Step 2
Bee's stripes, eyes and sting

Step 3
Wings

Diagram 2 – Constructing the bag

5mm (¹/4in) seam allowance

Voile

Seam with seam allowance pressed open

Linen

2.5cm (1in) 2.5cm (1in)

Machine-stitch leaving an opening in the voile.

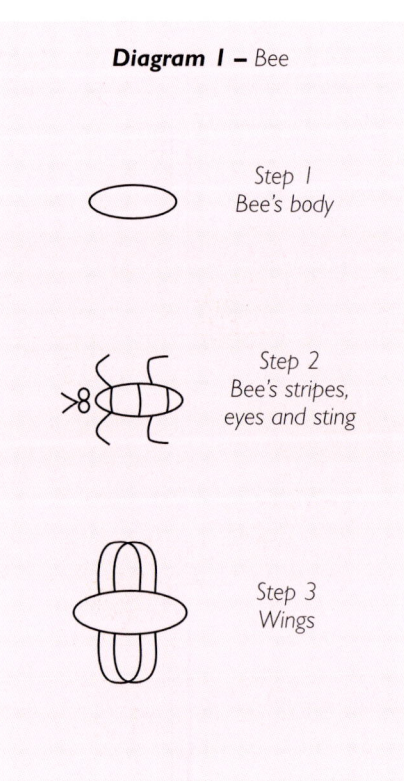

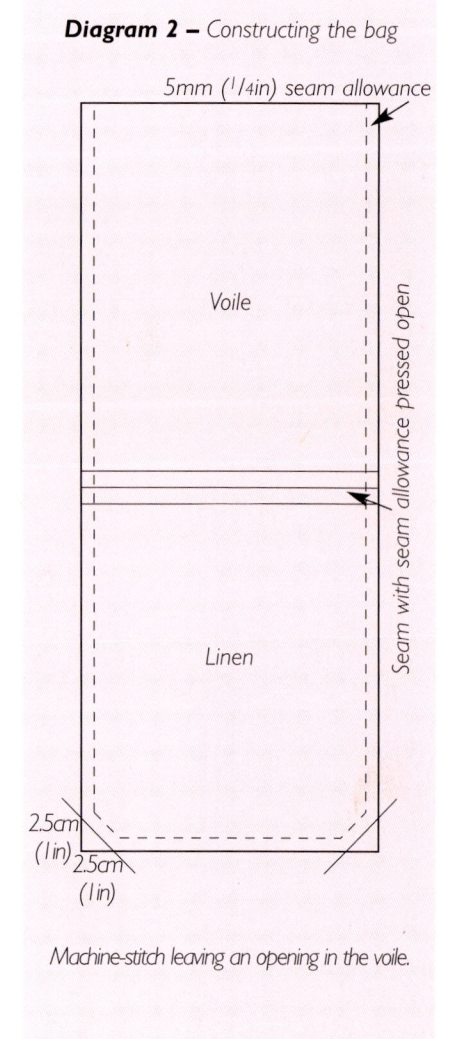

FINISHING

With the two pieces of linen right sides up, place the two remaining pieces of voile on top and pin them along the top raw edge only. Machine-stitch following the pins with a 5mm (¹/4in) seam allowance and press the seam open. Using a stiletto or knitting needle first to form the hole and make stitching easier, embroider the four eyelets with two strands of light brown grey (3023) in Buttonhole Stitch. Open up the joined linen and voile and place them right sides together but don't pin across the narrow side of the voile as this is left open for turning the bag right side out. Pin them together and machine-stitch them with a 5mm (¹/4in) seam allowance, following diagram 2. Push the bag through the opening in the voile to turn the embroidery to the outside. Trim the voile to measure 16.5cm (6¹/2in) in length, then turn it to the inside together with 4.5cm (1³/4in) of the linen to form the lining and casing. Work two rows of machine-stitching, 2cm (³/4in) and 3.5cm (1³/8in) from the turned-over top edge. Turn the voile out, fold the raw edges to the inside and stitch them neatly to finish off.

Using gold metallic thread (5282), make two twisted cords each 60cm (23³/4in) in length and thread them through the casing.

For further information, contact Joan Watters, phone 0412 518 989. ★

EMBROIDERY TREASURES — *Native Delights*

The Basic Essentials

The right tools are essential for any job – and needlework is no exception. There are a few essentials and some optional extras that every needleworker should have.

SCISSORS

❖

Buy the best you can afford and look after them. Good scissors will last you a lifetime. Look for scissors that can be unscrewed and sharpened professionally. Never – ever! – cut paper with scissors intended to cut fabric or thread. In fact, don't use them to cut anything but fabric or thread. Make sure the family knows your scissors are not for general use. If necessary, hide them!

Embroidery scissors should have fine blades tapering to sharp points as you will use them for cutting threads close to the fabric you are working on.

Take care not to damage the points by dropping the scissors. A scissor ball is a good idea. This is a small weight that attaches to the handles and ensures that the ball and not the points land first if the scissors are dropped.

You will also need a good pair of dressmaking scissors for cutting fabric. These should have long blades and comfortable handles. It is also a good idea to buy or make a sheath to store the scissors when not in use to avoid damage to the points.

HOOPS

There are various kinds of hoops on the market and the one you use is largely a matter of choice. They are all designed to keep your fabric taut so there is no puckering when you stitch. It is recommended that you always remove your embroidery from the hoop when you are not actually working on it. Fabric left in a hoop for a long time may develop marks that are difficult – sometimes even impossible – to remove.

The most popular style is the wooden hoop with a screw for tightening or loosening. They come in a variety of sizes from 10cm (4in) to 30cm (12in). To make sure the fabric is firmly gripped in the hoop, wrap the inner hoop with bias binding, which not only helps prevent the fabric slipping, but will also reduce the risk of marking the fabric.

Plastic spring hoops are useful for techniques that don't need the fabric to be held drum tight. They are light and convenient to use and there is no risk of snagging your fabric.

FRAMES

Some embroiderers prefer frames to hoops, particularly if working on a large area. Scroll frames come in a range of sizes, allowing a large rectangular surface to be worked on. The width of your fabric is determined by the width of the webbing or tape attached to the rollers at the top and bottom of the frame. If working a very long project such as a bellpull, the excess fabric can be wound around the top and bottom rollers, keeping a firm tension.

Stretcher frames are made up of wooden stretcher bars which are slotted together at the corners. Frames of different sizes can be made by combining different-sized bars.

Lightweight plastic frames with a semicircular piece that snaps over a round tube are also available. These come in modular style and can be made up to various sizes, square and rectangular. As these frames can be taken apart, they are quite convenient for travelling.

FABRIC MARKERS

There is a wide range of markers available. Some use permanent ink which will not wash out. Others are temporary markers – some are water-erasable and others fade with exposure to light. Before marking out a design, consider which variety will best suit your purpose. Markings made by pens that fade with light may disappear before your project is finished. A water-soluble marker may not be suitable for use on a fabric that cannot be washed. Always test your chosen marker on a scrap of the project fabric before marking out a whole design.

THIMBLES

Some embroiderers can't take a stitch without one, others won't wear them. Thimbles are very much a matter of personal preference. They range from the economy models to sterling silver and gold-plated keepsakes and beautiful antique examples of craftmanship from a more elegant age. There are also ornamental thimbles which are designed to be admired rather than used.

Thimbles are particularly useful when working on heavy fabrics.

STILETTOS

Also called an awl, this is a sharp-pointed instrument used to make a hole in heavy or stiff fabric. It is useful in ribbon embroidery to allow the ribbon to pass through the fabric without being crushed.

NEEDLES

There are many, many needles – all of them designed for a specific purpose. It is important to use the correct needle for the particular technique you are working. The size of the needle is governed by the thickness of the thread used. As a general rule, the thread should fit smoothly through the eye. Project instructions usually specify the size and type of needle to use and you should follow these recommendations for the best result.

The numbering on needles refers to the size of the needle. The larger the number, the finer the needle. The most commonly used embroidery needles are crewel, chenille, straw or milliner's and tapestry needles.

Crewel needles are the most frequently used embroidery needles. They have a sharp point so they can pierce the fabric easily and a long slim eye to take one or more threads of stranded cotton or wool. They come in sizes 1 to 10.

Straw or milliner's needles are long and the same width along the entire length of the shank. They are particularly suitable for bullion and knot stitches. They have a small, round eye which is easy to thread. Sizes range from 1 to 9.

Chenille needles have a sharp point and long eye, making them perfect for working thicker threads and particularly suitable for candlewicking and ribbon embroidery.

They come in sizes 13 to 26. Tapestry needles have a blunt point and are most frequently used for canvaswork and cross stitch on evenweave fabrics. The blunt point passes easily through the holes in the canvas or fabric and is unlikely to pierce any thread sharing a common hole. They are also used in whipped stitches as they will slip between the fabric and stitch without catching on the fabric and snagging it. Sizes range from 18 to 26.

FABRICS

❖

Linen, cotton, homespun or calico, silk, satin, damask and even lightweight fabrics like voile are suitable for hand embroidery. The purpose of the finished embroidery determines which fabric to use. Basically, the fabric must have enough body to support the weight of the embroidery and the weave should be firm enough to hold the thread.

A sheer fabric like voile requires a fine thread and care should be taken to avoid threads on the back showing through to the front and causing a shadow effect.

Another point to consider when choosing fabric is whether your fabric has a matt or shiny finish and whether there is sufficient contrast between the fabric and the threads to be used.

Linen, calico and damask can be laundered. Silk and satin may require dry-cleaning. Any fabric with a tendency to fray – linen and silk particularly – should be overlocked or overcast by hand before you commence your embroidery. Another alternative is to use an anti-fray product.

Velvet and velveteen offer a rich background, particularly for ribbon embroidery. Dress-weight fabrics have a base cloth that is not too closely woven and allows the ribbon to pass through easily. When working with threads on plush fabrics, care must be taken that the thread is thick enough to sit on the surface of the pile and not disappear into it.

Wool, cotton and linen are all suitable for embroidery with either ribbon or thread. Look for fabrics that are woven firmly enough to hold the threads. If using a loosely woven fabric you may need to add a backing to stabilise it and to prevent the stitches on the reverse side showing through to the front.

Silk is a luxurious background for special projects; moiré, dupion, Thai silk, taffeta, shot taffeta and satin are all suitable weights for items such as framed pictures, cushions, clothing and a variety of fashion accessories.

THREADS

❖

Stranded cottons, sometimes called floss, are probably the most popular of all embroidery threads. They come in an extensive range of colours and, although most are colour-fast, it is a good idea to test for colour-fastness if you are making something that will require washing. Stranded cottons are composed of six threads and can be used whole or separated into the number of strands required. If you are separating them, cut the required length, then separate one length at a time. Hold up the thread and allow it to untwist before putting together the number of threads you require. This helps the thread to sit well on the fabric and also prevents twisting and tangling. You can also blend two or more colours to create subtle shading. Stranded cottons come in a range of plain colours as well as variegated shades.

There are also stranded threads in pure silk and synthetics. These have a rich lustre and can be used whole, separated or blended as for stranded cottons.

Rayon threads are used for Brazilian embroidery and have a lustrous finish. They need to be handled differently from other threads and the instructions for Brazilian embroidery projects usually include this information.

Wools come in tapestry and crewel weights. If a finer wool is needed, use crewel wool rather than trying to split tapestry wool. Both come in a huge range of colours.

Perlé or pearl thread is a pure cotton two-ply, twisted to produce a beaded effect, available in weights from a thick No 3 through the middle weights, No 5 and 8, to a fine No 12. These have a good lustre and come in a wide colour range, but not all colours are available in all weights.

Hand-dyed threads are available in wool, silk and cotton, in both plain colours and overdyes. If the project is likely to require more than one skein of these threads, make sure you purchase the same dye lot, as when hand-dyed, the colours may vary between the various dye lots.

RIBBONS

❖

Pure silk ribbon is soft and pliable, with a surface that looks the same on both sides. Available in widths from 2mm up to 32mm with the most used widths being 2mm, 4mm and 7mm.

Sheer ribbons, such as the synthetic organdies, can be used alone or combined with another ribbon. They can be used to create shadow effects that lend perspective to your work and are suitable for folding as well as embroidery.

Synthetic ribbons made of 100 per cent Azlon look like silk ribbons, but they have more spring than silk and will not lie as flat against the fabric. Available in 3.5mm and 7mm widths in a wide range of plain colours, there is also a range of

EMBROIDERY TREASURES　　　　　　　　　The Basic Essentials

Azlon ombre ribbon in the 3.5mm width and a picot-edged 6mm polyester ombre ribbon. Plain polyester ribbons also come in many colours and widths.

Double-sided polyester satin comes in widths from 1.5mm to 90mm. It is heavier and shinier than silk ribbon and suitable for making folded roses, concertina roses, free-form flowers, buds and leaves. The narrowest satin ribbon can be couched to form branches and stems.

The use of a stiletto is recommended if you wish to use polyester satin ribbon for embroidery. ✶

Stitch Guide

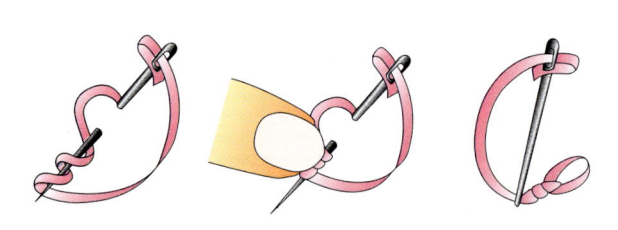

BULLION LAZY DAISY STITCH
Begin by working a Lazy Daisy Stitch to the point where the small holding stitch is about to be completed. Take the needle through the fabric on the other side of the loop as though to complete the stitch, and bring it back up again within the loop, next to the previous stitch. Do not pull the needle through yet. Now, make the Bullion Stitch, holding the coiled thread in place with the thumb. While holding the coil in place, take the needle to the back of the fabric on the other side of the loop.

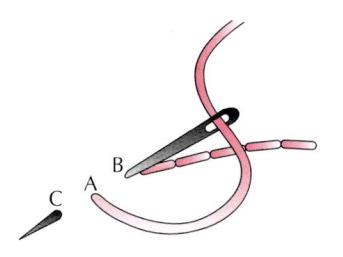

BACK STITCH
Bring the needle up at A. Take a small stitch backwards and go down at B, sliding the needle to come out at C. The distance between A and B, and A and C should be equal.

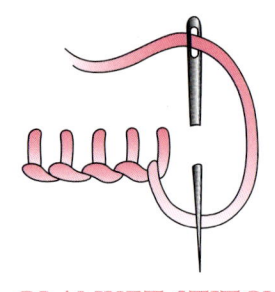

BLANKET STITCH
Bring the thread out on the lower line, insert the needle in position in the upper line, taking a straight downward stitch with the thread under the needle point. Pull up the stitch to form a loop and repeat.

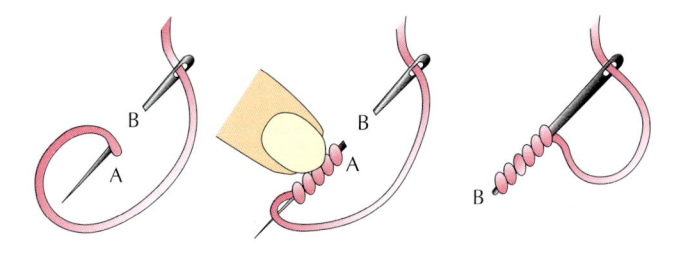

BULLION STITCH
Bring the needle up at A and go down at B leaving the loop of thread on the front of the work. Bring the needle partially through the fabric at A. Wrap the needle with the loop thread (doing as many wraps as equals the distance between A and B). Gently draw the needle through the twists and use it to hold the bullion against the fabric as you pull the thread through. Take the needle to the back again at B and give a firm pull to tighten up the knot.

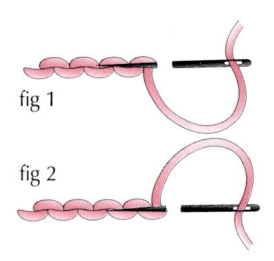

CABLE STITCH
This stitch is worked from left to right. Fig 1 – bring the thread through on the line of the design. Insert the needle a little to the right on the line and bring the needle out to the left midway between the length of the stitch, with the thread below the needle. Fig 2 – work the next stitch in the same way, but with the thread above the needle. Continue in this way, alternating the position of the thread. This stitch may also be worked on evenweave fabric.

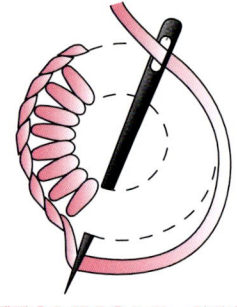

BUTTONHOLE STITCH
This is worked the same way as Blanket Stitch, except the stitches are worked very close together. It is sometimes used for finishing scalloped edges or in cutwork. Also used for a decorative edging with the vertical stitches worked alternately long and short.

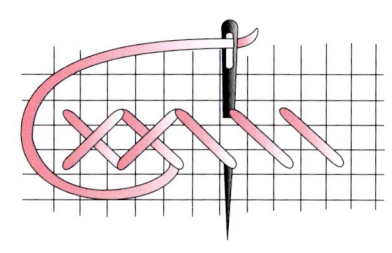

CROSS STITCH

Usually worked on evenweave fabric. Bring the needle up at the lower right-hand side. Take the needle up and across the same number of threads (up two and across two is the most usual). Stitch to the end of the row, forming a row of half crosses. Work back in the opposite direction, completing the cross. This stitch may be worked right to left or left to right, whichever you prefer, but it is essential that all the top crosses lie in the same direction.

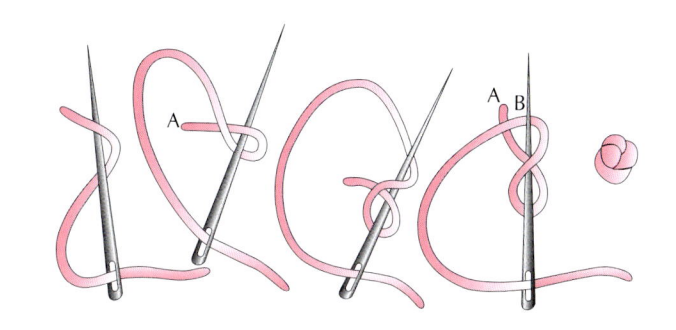

COLONIAL KNOT

Bring the needle up at A. Manipulate the needle to wrap the thread over, under, over and under the needle forming a figure '8'. Go back through the fabric at B (as close as possible to A). Keep the needle vertical while tightening the thread firmly around the needle. Hold the knot in place as you pull the thread through to the back.

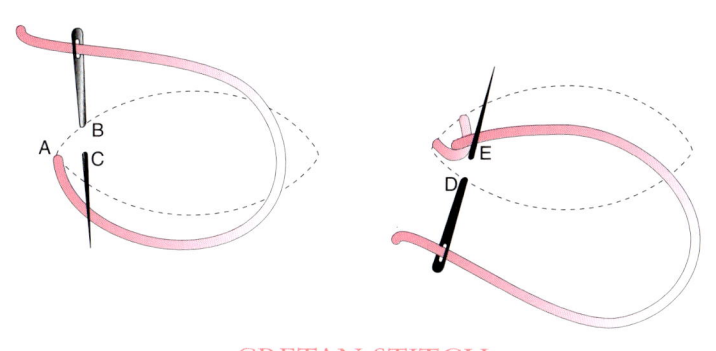

CRETAN STITCH

Bring the needle to the front of the fabric at point A. Take a small stitch in at B and coming out at C. The thread should be under the needle and the needle should face the centre of the shape to be filled. Turn the needle around, insert it at D and come out at E, again keep the thread under the needlepoint. Continue alternating the sides until the shape is completely filled.

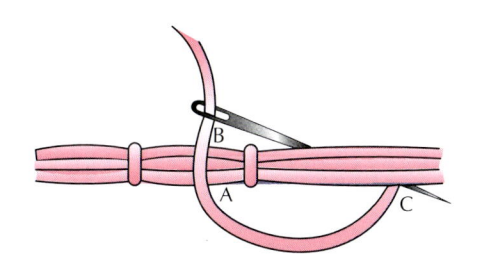

COUCHING STITCH

Couching is used to attach threads to the surface of the fabric. It is often used to attach threads too thick or textured to be stitched through the fabric. Bring out the thread to be Couched at the start of the stitching line. Remove the needle and hold the thread in place with your thumb. Thread another needle with the Couching thread and bring it up on the stitching line at A. Take a small stitch over the laid thread at B, bringing the needle up again at C. Repeat to the end of the stitching line, keeping your Couching Stitches evenly spaced. Rethread the Couched thread and take it through to the back of the work and fasten off.

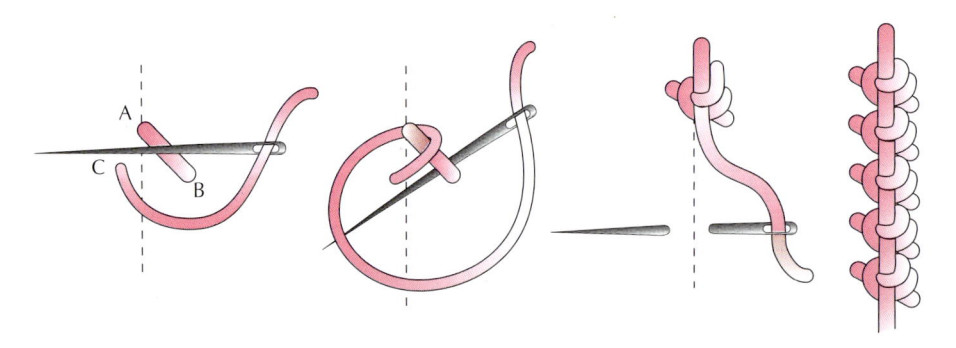

DOUBLE KNOT STITCH

This stitch is also known as a Palestrina Knot Stitch. Bring the threaded needle from the back of the fabric to the front at point A. Take a small stitch to point B and re-enter the fabric at point C. Slip the needle under the stitch made between points A and B, making sure not to pierce the fabric. Taking the same direction, slip the needle under this stitch again. The needlepoint should stay on top of the threaded loop. Pull the needle through to form the knot.

FEATHER STITCH

Bring the needle up at A and go down at B – even with and to the left of A – and emerge at C. Alternate the stitches back and forth, working them downwards in a vertical column. (Double Feather Stitch is worked the same way, except that two stitches are worked before the direction is changed.)

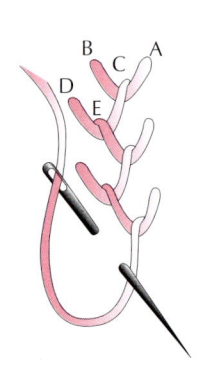

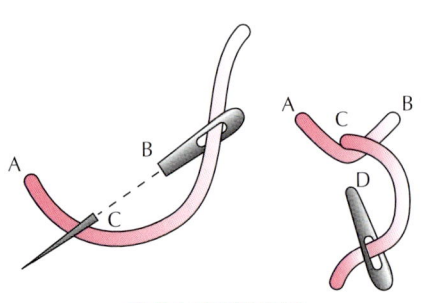

FLY STITCH

Bring the needle up at A and go down at B (to the right of and level with A), coming up again at C with the tip of the needle over the thread or ribbon. Pull the thread through the fabric and go to the back of the work again at D. This stitch can be used singly or stacked one on top of the other. The stitch from C to D can be quite small or extended.

FOLDED RIBBON ROSES

1. Fold raw edge down a little, then roll ribbon three or four times to form centre of rose.

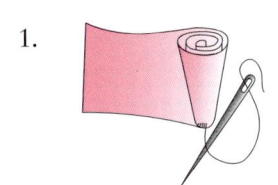

2. Fold ribbon on the cross. Each fold of ribbon is a petal.

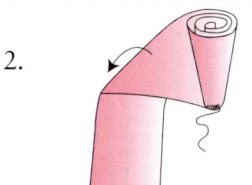

3. Pull centre of rose down so when you roll it into the ribbon it will be level with the top of the fold. Stitch the base of the rose after each fold.

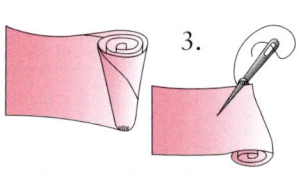

4. Keep folding and stitching until you have the size and shape you want. To finish, stitch the ribbon at the bottom of the rose to prevent fraying.

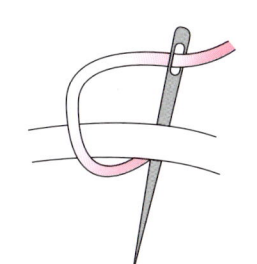

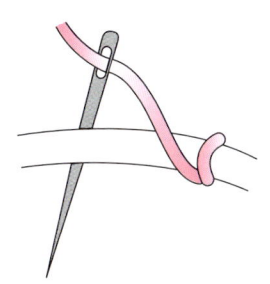

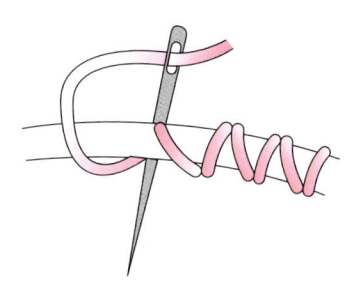

GLOVE STITCH

Draw two parallel lines. Bring the needle up at A and down at B to make a Straight Stitch. Bring the needle out again at A and down at C. Try to keep the stitches even

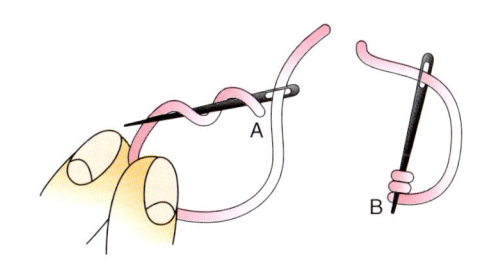

FRENCH KNOTS

Bring the needle up at A and wrap the thread around the needle twice (or required number of times). Holding the thread firmly, go down at B (as close as possible to A, without actually going through the same hole). The knot should be held in place while the needle is pulled completely through to the back of the fabric.

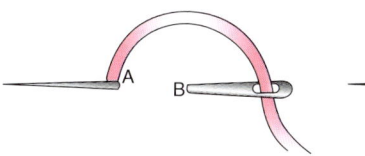

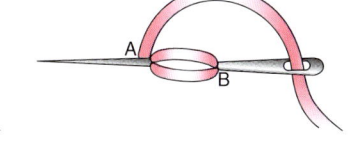

GRANITOS STITCH

Begin by working a small Straight Stitch. Make a few more Straight Stitches, being careful to enter and exit in the same hole as the first stitch.

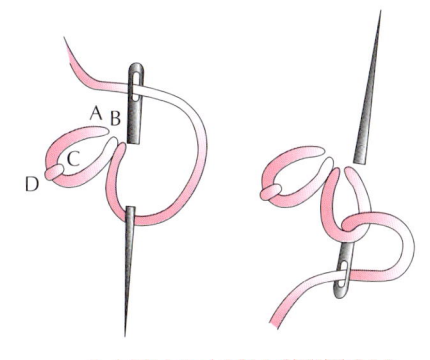

LAZY DAISY STITCH (DETACHED CHAIN)

Bring the needle up at A. Slide the needle from B (as close as possible to A, but not actually through the same hole) through to C, taking the tip of the needle over the loop formed. Go down at D, creating a holding stitch.

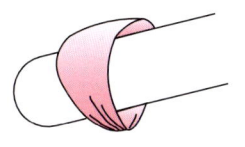

LOOP STITCH

Bring the needle through to the right side of the fabric at the required point. Holding the ribbon against the fabric, take the needle back through to the wrong side at the same point it emerged, until a small loop of ribbon is left on the right side. Take care that the ribbon does not twist, so that the loop remains smooth. To ensure every loop is identical, slip a knitting needle inside the loop of ribbon as it is tightened. Once the ribbon sits neatly around the knitting needle, it can be removed.

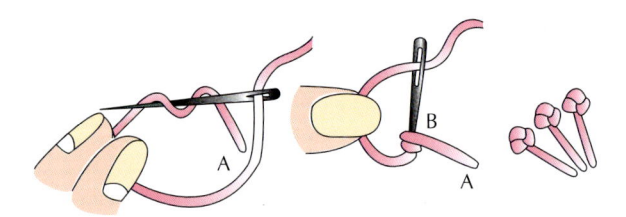

PISTIL STITCH

Bring the needle up at A and, at the desired length of your stitch, wrap twice around the needle, as for French Knot. Go back into the fabric at B, holding the knot in place as you take the needle and thread completely through the fabric.

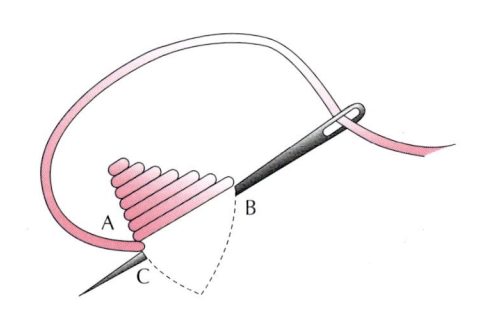

SATIN STITCH

Bring the needle up at A, go down at B and slide the needle through to C. Continue working in this manner, keeping the stitches parallel and close together until the shape has been filled.

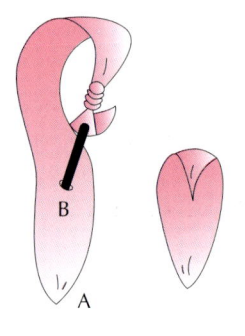

RIBBON STITCH

Bring the needle up at A and lay the ribbon flat on the fabric. Put the needle into the middle of the ribbon at B and pull carefully through the fabric, making the edges of the ribbon curl towards to tip. Do not pull too tightly.

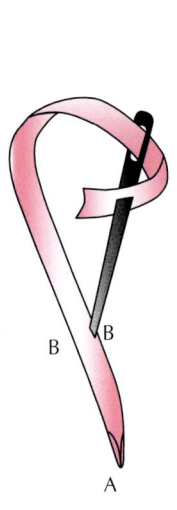

SIDE RIBBON STITCH

Bring the needle up at A and lay the ribbon flat on the fabric. Re-insert the needle at either the right side or the left side of the ribbon at B and pull the needle carefully through the ribbon and fabric, making the edges of the ribbon curl. Do not pull too tightly.

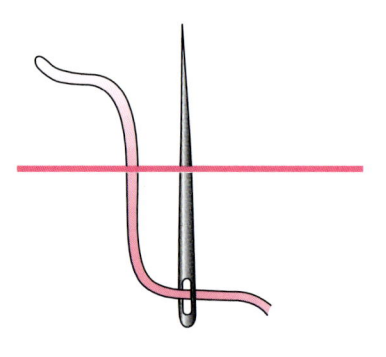

STAB STITCH

Similar to Straight Stitch, this stitch is worked in a stabbing motion. That is, the threaded needle is taken through the fabric and pulled through before the next stitch is taken. This is useful if the fabric is thick or if there are many layers.

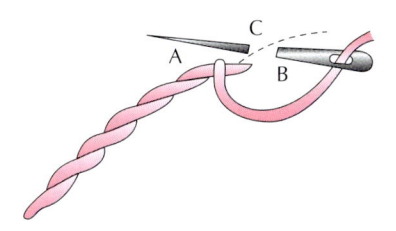

STEM STITCH
Work from left to right. Keep the thread down below the needle, come up at A and go back down into the fabric at B, coming out again at C (which should be halfway along the length of the previous stitch).

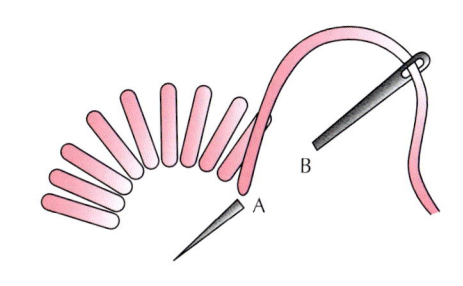

STRAIGHT STITCH
Bring the needle up at A, go down at B. Straight stitches should be fairly firm so that they lie flat on the fabric and not too long or they may catch. They can be worked in any direction and various lengths.

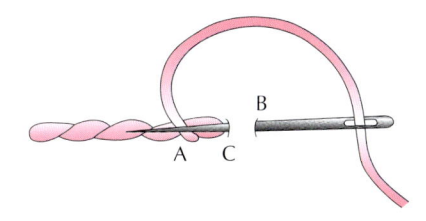

STEM STITCH (THREAD UP)
Work from left to right. Keep the thread above the needle, come up at A and go back onto the fabric at B, coming out again at C (which should be halfway along the length of the previous stitch).

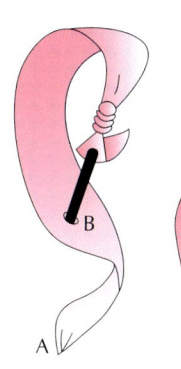

TWISTED RIBBON STITCH
Work this stitch as for Ribbon Stitch by bringing the needle threaded with ribbon to the front at A. Twist the ribbon back to front, and then continue to enter at B. Do not pull too tightly.

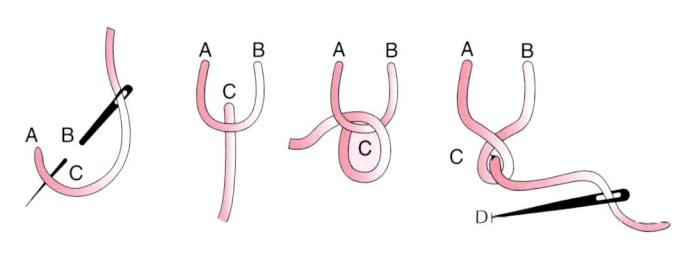

TWISTED FLY STITCH
Bring the needle up at A and go down at B (to the right of and level with A), coming up again at C, with the tip of the needle under the thread or ribbon. Pull the thread through the fabric leaving a small loop, then pass the needle and thread over and through the looped thread, to twist the loop as shown. Work the holding stitch over the looped part of the stitch to D.

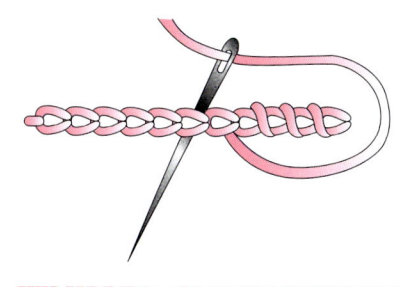

WHIPPED CHAIN STITCH
Work a foundation row of Chain Stitch. A second thread is used to whip at regular intervals. Bring the needle to the front, then whip over from right to left then under each stitch, without picking up the ground fabric. The whipping stitches should fall neatly over the junction of each stitch. Use a blunt ended tapestry needle for the second thread to avoid splitting the stitches in the foundation row.

Index

Adams, Judith 38
Back Stitch 51, 54, 62, 70, 74, 81
Bennett, Jennifer 61
blackwork 69
blanket 34
Blanket Stitch 54
bookmark 53
bowl 44
Bullion Lazy Daisy Stitch 58
Bullion Stitch 9, 18, 32, 45
Buttonhole Stitch 35, 81
Cable Stitch 39
cake band 50
candlewicking 22
Cashion, Maxeen 73
chatelaine 61
Colonial Knot 23, 58, 81
Couching 45
Cretan Stitch 23
Cross Stitch 50, 51, 53, 54, 73, 74
cushion 12, 57
Double Knot Stitch
(Palestrina Knot Stitch) 23, 62, 63
Edwards, Marian 22
embroidery, Brazilian 44
embroidery, fine 8, 17, 76
embroidery, history 4
embroidery, tips 13, 18, 35, 45, 66, 84
embroidery, wool 12, 13, 34, 35, 57
fabric markers 85
fabrics 86
Feather Stitch 23
Fly Stitch, 18, 32, 58, 62, 81
Folded Ribbon Rose 32

framed pieces 17, 31, 65, 73
frames 85
French Knots 13, 18, 32, 35, 45, 58
Garforth, Vivienne 53
Glove Stitch 77
Granitos Stitch 58, 77
greeting card 53
Gryllis, Linda 69
Hanauer, Rosemarie 57
handtowel 8
Hardanger 53
hoops 85
Kelley, Debbie 44
Kloster Blocks 54
Lazy Daisy Stitch 9, 18, 32, 35, 39, 58, 81
Liz and Pauline Designs 12
Loop Stitch 32
McNeice, Jan 34
needles 85
One-step Wave Stitch 39
Palestrina Knot Stitch
(Double Knot Stitch) 23, 62, 63
pincushion 38
Pistil Stitch 32, 58
placemat 69
Ribbon Stitch 32, 62, 66

ribbonwork 31, 65, 80
ribbons 86
Rich, Robyn 17
Ricketts, Sarah 50
sachets 22, 80
Satin Stitch 13, 35, 45, 54, 77
Scissors 84
Side Ribbon Stitch 66
Smocking 38
Stab Stitch 81
Stair-step Wave 39
Stem Stitch 9, 13, 18, 35, 45, 58, 66, 77
stilettos 85
Straight Stitch 9, 13, 18, 35, 45, 58, 62, 66
Sumner, Christine 31
tape measure cover 76
thimbles 85
threads 86
tassel 63
Turkey Stitch 62
Twisted Fly Stitch 58
Twisted Straight Stitch 66
Watson, Angela 8
Watters, Joan 80
Whipped Chain Stitch 77
Young, Wendie 65, 76

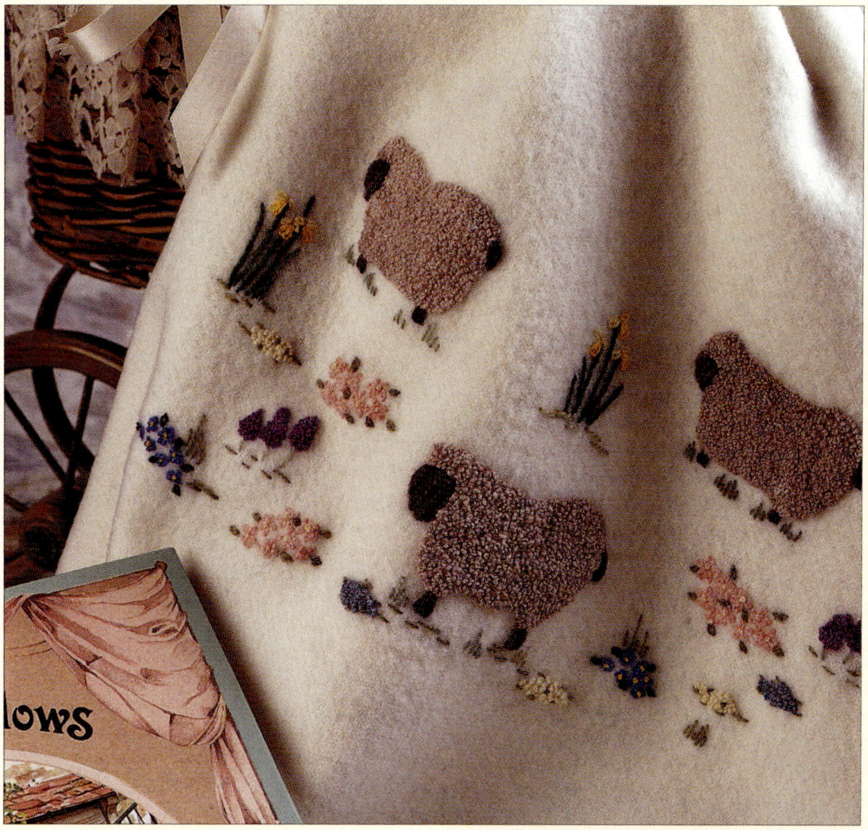
lows

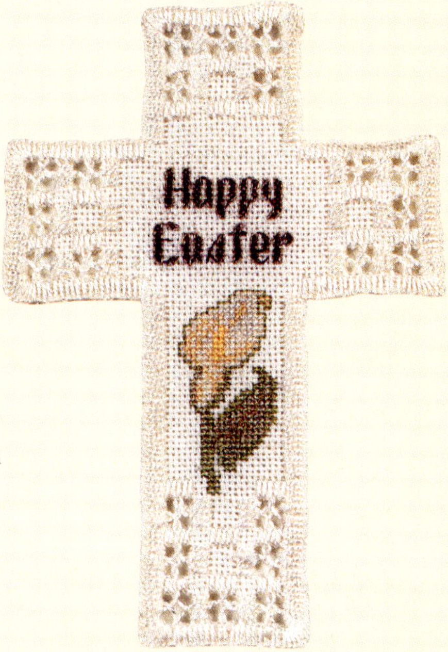
Happy
Easter

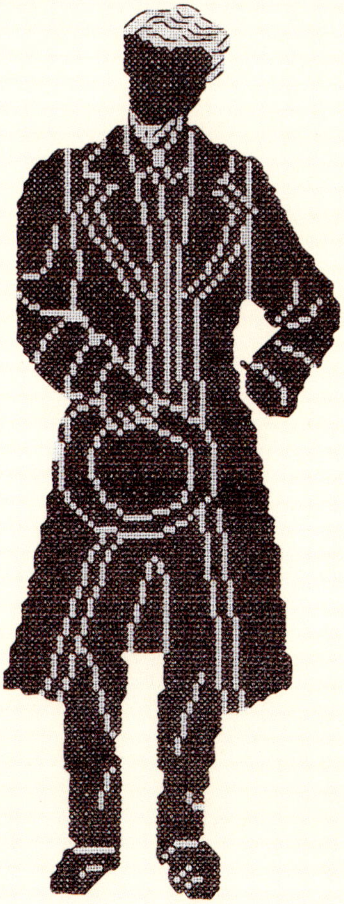

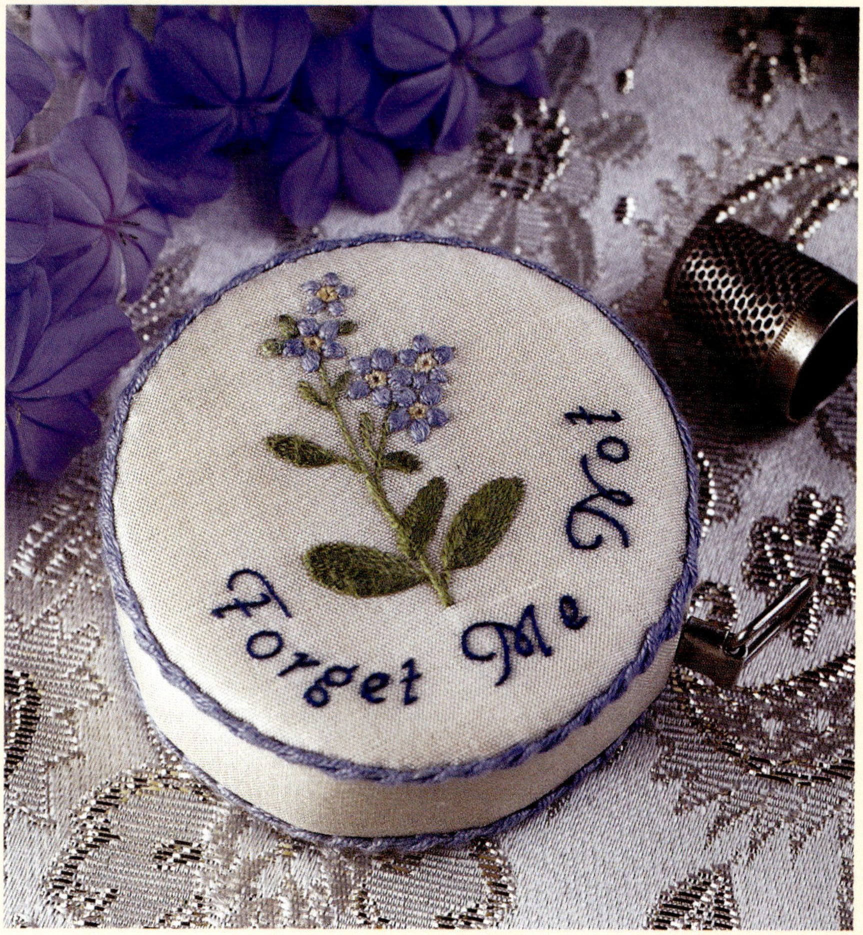
Forget Me Not

Published by Craftworld Books
A division of Express Publications Pty Ltd. ACN 057 807 904
Under licence from EP Investments Pty Ltd, ACN 003 109 055 (1995)

2 Stanley Street
Silverwater NSW 2128
Australia

First published by Craftworld Books 2001
Copyright Text and illustrations: Express Publications Pty Ltd 2001
Copyright Published edition: Craftworld Books 2001

All rights reserved. Without limiting the rights under the above copyrights, no part of this publication may be reproduced, stored in a retrieval system or transmitted by any means, whether electronic, mechanical or otherwise without the prior written consent of the publisher.

Publisher Sue Aiken
Photographic Director Robyn Wilson
Editor Sylvia Kalan
Associate Editor Judith Adams
Production Editor Gabrielle Baxter
Designer Natasha Hayles

Photographer Tim Connolly
Stylist Robyn Wilson

National Library of Australia Cataloguing-in-Publication data

Embroidery Treasures

Includes Index
ISBN 1 875625 30 5

1. Embroidery 2. Decoration and ornament

Printed by KHL Printing
Australia Distribution to newsagents by Network Distribution Company, 54 Park Street, Sydney NSW 2000 Ph (02) 9282 8777

Overseas Distribution Enquiries Godfrey Vella Ph (02) 9748 0599, Locked Bag 111, Silverwater NSW 1811 Australia

Email: gvella@expresspublications.com.au